LONGMAN
KEYSTONE

B

Reader's Companion Workbook

Anna Uhl Chamot

John De Mado

Sharroky Hollie

PEARSON
Longman

KEYSTONE

Keystone B Reader's Companion Workbook

Copyright © by Pearson Education, Inc.

All rights reserved. No part of this publication may be reproduced, stored in a retrieval system, or transmitted in any form or by any means, electronic, mechanical, photocopying, recording, or otherwise, without the prior permission of the publisher.

Pearson Education, 10 Bank Street, White Plains, NY 10606

Staff credits: The people who made up the *Longman Keystone* team, representing editorial, production, design, manufacturing, and marketing are John Ade, Rhea Banker, Liz Barker, Danielle Belfiore, Don Bensey, Virginia Bernard, Kenna Bourke, Anne Boynton-Trigg, Johnnie Farmer, Maryann Finocchi, Patrice Fraccio, Geraldine Geniusas, Charles Green, Henry Hild, David L. Jones, Lucille M. Kennedy, Ed Lamprich, Emily Lippincott, Tara Maceyak, Maria Pia Marrella, Linda Moser, Laurie Neaman, Sherri Pemberton, Liza Pleva, Joan Poole, Edie Pullman, Monica Rodriguez, Tania Saiz-Sousa, Chris Siley, Lynn Sobotta, Heather St. Clair, Jennifer Stem, Siobhan Sullivan, Jane Townsend, Heather Vomero, Marian Wassner, Lauren Weidenman, Matthew Williams, and Adina Zoltan.

Cover Image: Background, John Foxx/Getty Images; Inset, Sandra Dionisi/Getty Images
Text composition: TSI Graphics
Text font: 11 pt ITC Stone Sans Std
Photos: 14 Dorling Kindersley; 15 Greg Baker/AP/Wide World Photos; 19 top-left, Digital Vision/Getty Images; top-right, Nicholas Devore III/Still Media; bottom-left, Ken Findlay/Dorling Kindersley; bottom-right, Gregory Ochocki/Photo Researchers, Inc.; 24 Alan Hills/Dorling Kindersley/© The British Museum; 26 Dorling Kindersley; 28 Peter Dennis/Dorling Kindersley; 31 Bildarchiv Preussischer Kulturbesitz/Art Resource, NY; 39 Tom Walker; 40 Nigel Marven/Nature Picture Library; 43 Joel Sartore/National Geographic Image Collection; 53 Art Resource, NY/Centre Pompidou/Frida Kahlo (1907–1954). *The Frame*, Self-Portrait, (ca. 1937–38). Oil on aluminum, under glass and painted wood, 28.5 × 20.5 cm. © Banco de Mexico Diego Rivera & Frida Kahlo Museums Trust. Av. Cinco de Mayo No. 2, Col. Centro, Del. Cuauhtemoc 06059; 59 Faridodin Lajvardi/Carl Hayden Community HS Website; 65 Faridodin Lajvardi/Carl Hayden Community HS Website; 79 Dave King/Dorling Kindersley/Courtesy of Phil Farrand; 89 Bettmann/CORBIS; 95 Bettmann/CORBIS; 105 National Museum of American History, Smithsonian Institution; 111 Courtesy of the Library of Congress; 112 Bettmann/CORBIS; 114 Geoff Brightling/Dorling Kindersley; 115 Randy Wells/Stone Allstock/Getty Images; 124 Jean-Charles Cuillandre/CFHT/Photo Researchers, Inc.; 125 Sachsische Landesbibliothek/Fagan, People of the Earth, 11/ed, 2004; 126 Dagli Orti/Museo Nazionale Romano Rome/The Art Archive; 131 Peter Bull/Dorling Kindersley; 140 Peter Bull/Dorling Kindersley; 142 Yann Arthus-Bertrand/CORBIS; 145 Peter Bull/Dorling Kindersley.
Illustrations: Inklink Firenze, 6; John Hovell, 77; Mapping Specialists, 99, 101, 119
Technical art: TSI Graphics
Acknowledgements:
"Ecosystems: The Systems of Nature." Copyright © Pearson Longman, 10 Bank Street, White Plains, NY 10606.
"Water and Living Things." Copyright © Pearson Longman, 10 Bank Street, White Plains, NY 10606.
"Early Explorers." Copyright © Pearson Longman, 10 Bank Street, White Plains, NY 10606.
"Migrating Caribou." Copyright © Pearson Longman, 10 Bank Street, White Plains, NY 10606.
Excerpt from *Magnetism* by Darlene R. Stilla. Copyright © 2005 by The Child's World®. Reprinted by permission.
"Success Stories." Copyright © Pearson Longman, 10 Bank Street, White Plains, NY 10606.
"Students Win Robotics Competition" by Karina Bland. Published as "Robot Victory Just Part of Story for Hayden Students" from *The Arizona Republic*, March 25, 2006. Reprinted by permission.
"Changing Earth." Copyright © Pearson Longman, 10 Bank Street, White Plains, NY 10606.
Excerpt from *Through My Eyes* by Ruby Bridges. Copyright © 1999 by Ruby Bridges. Reprinted by permission of Scholastic Inc.
"Maps and Compasses." Copyright © Pearson Longman, 10 Bank Street, White Plains, NY 10606.
"The Cowboy Era," adapted from *Cowboy*, Dorling Kindersley.
"Early Astronomers." Copyright © Pearson Longman, 10 Bank Street, White Plains, NY 10606.
Excerpt from *Prentice Hall Science; Explorer Earth Science* by M. J. Padilla, PhD., I. Miaoulis, PhD., and M. Cyr, PhD. Copyright © 2001 by Pearson Education, Inc. publishing or Prentice Hall. Used by permission.

ISBN-13: 978-0-13-612861-8
ISBN-10: 0-13-612861-0

PEARSON LONGMAN ON THE WEB

Pearsonlongman.com offers online resources for teachers and students. Access our Companion Websites, our online catalog, and our local offices around the world.

Visit us at **pearsonlongman.com**.

Printed in the United States of America
2 3 4 5 6 7 8 9 10 11—CRS—13 12 11 10 09 08

Contents

Unit 1

READING 2: "Ecosystems: The Systems of Nature"

Summary / Visual Summary 1
Reader's Companion 2
Reading Wrap-Up 8
Edit for Meaning 9
Focus on Details 11
Read for Fluency 12

READING 4: "Water and Living Things"

Summary / Visual Summary 13
Reader's Companion 14
Reading Wrap-Up 18
Edit for Meaning 19
Focus on Details 21
Read for Fluency 22

Unit 2

READING 2: "Early Explorers"

Summary / Visual Summary	23
Reader's Companion	24
Reading Wrap-Up	30
Edit for Meaning	31
Focus on Details	33
Read for Fluency	34

READING 3: "Migrating Caribou" / "Magnets in Animals"

Summary / Visual Summary	35
Reader's Companion	36
Reading Wrap-Up	42
Edit for Meaning	43
Focus on Details	45
Read for Fluency	46

Unit 3

READING 1: "Success Stories"

Summary / Visual Summary 47
Reader's Companion 48
Reading Wrap-Up 52
Edit for Meaning 53
Focus on Details 55
Read for Fluency 56

READING 4: "Students Win Robotics Competition"

Summary / Visual Summary 57
Reader's Companion 58
Reading Wrap-Up 64
Edit for Meaning 65
Focus on Details 67
Read for Fluency 68

Contents   **v**

Unit 4

READING 1: "Changing Earth"

Summary / Visual Summary 69
Reader's Companion 70
Reading Wrap-Up 78
Edit for Meaning 79
Focus on Details. 81
Read for Fluency 82

READING 3: From *Through My Eyes*

Summary / Visual Summary 83
Reader's Companion 84
Reading Wrap-Up 94
Edit for Meaning 95
Focus on Details. 97
Read for Fluency 98

Unit 5

READING 2: "Maps and Compasses"

Summary / Visual Summary. 99
Reader's Companion 100
Reading Wrap-Up 104
Edit for Meaning 105
Focus on Details. 107
Read for Fluency 108

READING 3: "The Cowboy Era"

Summary / Visual Summary. 109
Reader's Companion 110
Reading Wrap-Up 118
Edit for Meaning 119
Focus on Details. 121
Read for Fluency 122

Unit 6

READING 2: "Early Astronomers"

Summary / Visual Summary 123
Reader's Companion 124
Reading Wrap-Up 130
Edit for Meaning 131
Focus on Details. 133
Read for Fluency 134

READING 4: "Earth's Orbit"

Summary / Visual Summary 135
Reader's Companion 136
Reading Wrap-Up 144
Edit for Meaning 145
Focus on Details. 147
Read for Fluency 148

Name _____ Date _____

How does the natural world affect us?

READING 2: "Ecosystems: The Systems of Nature"

SUMMARY *Use with textbook pages 20–25.*

This passage tells how the different parts of nature work together. An ecosystem is made up of both the living things and the nonliving things in an area. Plants and animals are examples of living things. Rocks and water are examples of nonliving things. The passage tells about the different kinds of living things and the places, or habitats, they live in. It also explains that each member of the ecosystem is important to every other member.

Visual Summary

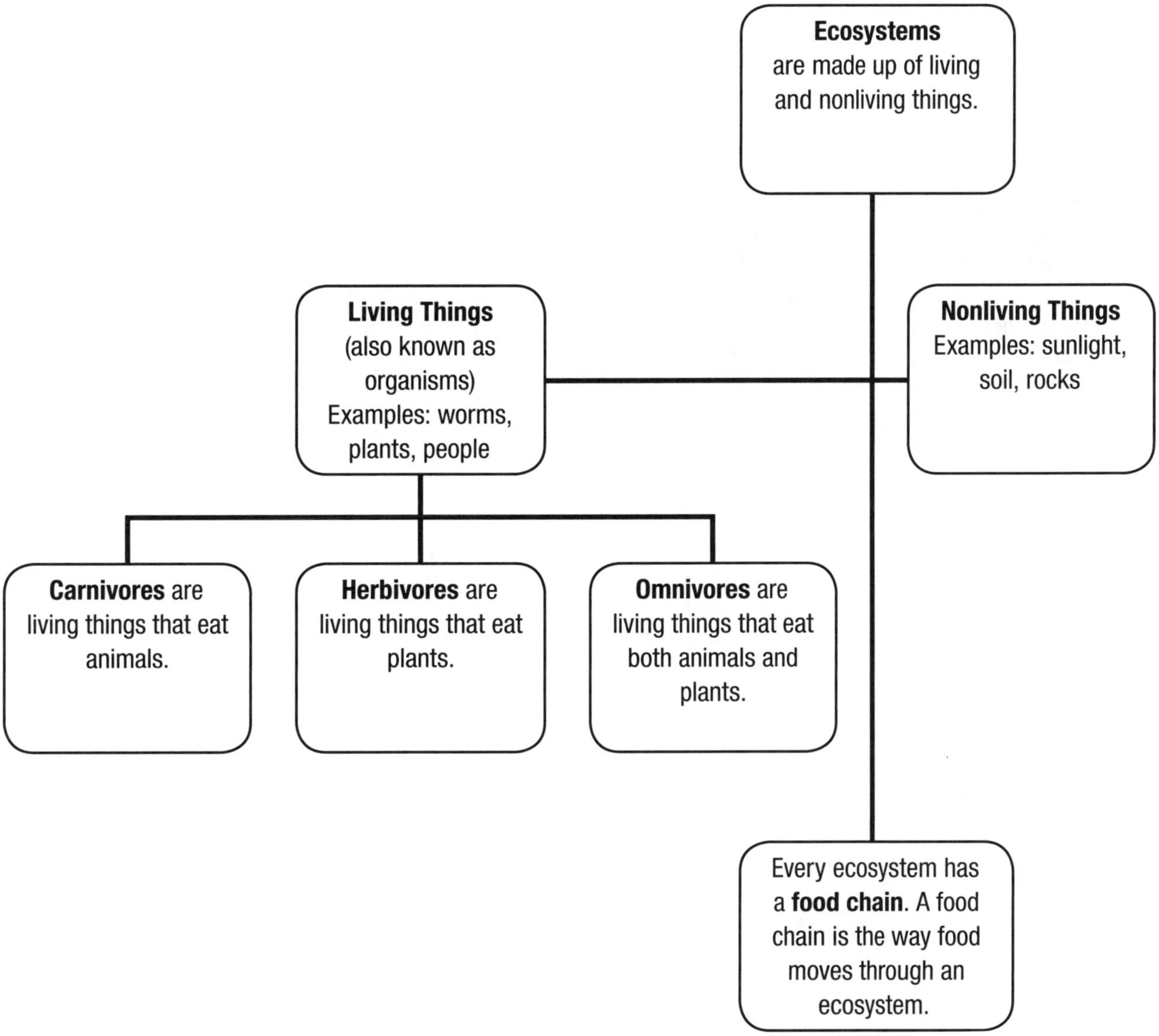

Ecosystems are made up of living and nonliving things.

Living Things (also known as organisms) Examples: worms, plants, people

Nonliving Things Examples: sunlight, soil, rocks

Carnivores are living things that eat animals.

Herbivores are living things that eat plants.

Omnivores are living things that eat both animals and plants.

Every ecosystem has a **food chain**. A food chain is the way food moves through an ecosystem.

Unit 1 • Reading 2

Use What You Know

Name three different kinds of organisms, or living things.

1. _____
2. _____
3. _____

Text Structure

The title tells what the article is about. Circle the title of the article. What might "The Systems of Nature" mean?

_____
_____
_____

Reading Strategy: Preview

Before reading the article, preview it by looking at the main title and headings of each section. Underline the headings. What do you think this article will be about?

_____
_____
_____

Ecosystems: The Systems of Nature

Organisms and Species

An organism is a living thing. A huge redwood tree is an organism. A small mouse is an organism. A tiny insect is an organism. A human is an organism, too. Some organisms, such as bacteria, are so small that you cannot see them.

A group of very similar organisms is a species. The organisms in a species are so similar that they can reproduce—that is, have offspring, or babies—together, and their offspring can reproduce, too. Horses and cows, for example, cannot have offspring together because they are different species.

Habitats

A habitat is the place where an organism lives—its surroundings or environment. A habitat provides the things an organism needs to survive, such as food, water, a livable temperature, and shelter. A habitat can be as large as an ocean or as small as a drop of water. It can be a forest or one tree. Several species may live in the same habitat, such as a river.

---

shelter, place that protects you from bad weather or danger

Name _____ Date _____

Different organisms live in different habitats because they have different requirements for survival. For example, a river or lake can be the habitat of some species of freshwater fish, such as trout. Freshwater trout cannot survive in the ocean, which contains salt water. An ocean and a lake are very different habitats. Similarly, the desert in the southwestern United States and northern Mexico is the habitat of the saguaro cactus. The saguaro cactus cannot survive in a tropical rain forest.

Sometimes animals move to different places within their habitats. For example, many kinds of frogs are born in water. However, they live mostly on land when they grow up. During very cold weather, some frogs go under the ground or bury themselves in mud at the bottom of ponds to stay warm.

requirements, needs
tropical, hot and wet
ponds, small lakes

Comprehension Check

Underline the reason why different organisms live in different habitats. Why would freshwater trout have trouble surviving in the ocean?

_____
_____
_____

Text Structure

Science textbooks often have bolded vocabulary words. Their definitions are at the bottom of the page. Circle one of the highlighted words on this page. Look at its definition. Reread the sentence in which it appears. Rewrite the sentence without using the word.

_____
_____
_____
_____

Comprehension Check

Underline the various places a frog may move within its habitat. Why would a frog live in one part of its habitat in summer and in another part in winter?

_____
_____
_____

Unit 1 • Reading 2

Reading Strategy: Preview

When you preview, you think about what you already know about the subject of the article. What do you think the difference is between a population and a community?

_____
_____
_____

Text Structure

A science article often explains important terms. Underline the definition of the term *population*. List three populations.

1. _____
2. _____
3. _____

Comprehension Check

Underline why different populations in a community interact with one another. Then give an example of how different animals use the same resources.

_____
_____
_____

Populations and Communities

All the members of one species in the same area are a population. For example, all the frogs in a lake are a population. All the pine trees in a forest are a population. All the people in a city, state, or country are a population. Some populations do not stay in one place. Monarch butterflies travel south each year from parts of western Canada and the United States to Mexico. Some species of whales travel around many oceans.

A community is all the populations that live together in one place, such as all the plants and animals in a desert. In a community, the different populations live close together, so they interact with one another. One way populations interact in a community is by using the same resources, such as food and shelter. In a desert, for example, snakes, lizards, and spiders may all use rocks and holes for shelter. They may eat insects, other animals, or their own kind of food.

Name _____ Date _____

The Parts of an Ecosystem

An ecosystem is made up of both the living and nonliving things in an area. Nonliving things include air, sunlight, water, rocks, and soil. All parts of an ecosystem, living and nonliving, interact. Plants take water from the soil, and they produce oxygen. Animals breathe in oxygen from the air. They eat plants and other animals.

Three Kinds of Organisms

In an ecosystem, there are three kinds of organisms: producers, consumers, and decomposers. Each kind of organism is important.

Most producers are plants. They use energy from sunlight to make their own food from water and carbon dioxide. (Carbon dioxide is a gas in the air. People and animals breathe it out.) This process of making food is called photosynthesis.

Consumers cannot make their own food. They eat, or consume, other organisms. All animals are consumers. Consumers are classified by what they eat.

- **Herbivores**, such as deer, horses, and many birds, eat only plants.
- **Carnivores**, such as lions, spiders, and snakes, eat only animals. Some carnivores are scavengers. A scavenger eats dead organisms. Scavengers include vultures and catfish.
- **Omnivores**, such as crows and bears, eat plants *and* animals.

---

soil, top layer of earth
oxygen, gas in the air that all plants and animals need to live
breathe, take air through the nose and mouth
energy, power that produces heat
classified, put into groups

Comprehension Check

Underline the sentence that defines what an ecosystem is made up of. What are some examples of nonliving things?

_____
_____
_____

Reading Strategy: Preview

Circle the word in the heading that tells you how many kinds of organisms you will be reading about. How does putting a number in a heading help you preview what is coming next?

_____
_____
_____

Comprehension Check

Circle the three different types of organisms. What is the difference between an herbivore and an omnivore?

_____
_____
_____

Unit 1 • Reading 2   5

Comprehension Check

Underline what decomposers do. Why is it good for the ecosystem that decomposers break down plants and animals?

_____
_____
_____

Text Structure

A paragraph contains a main idea. Circle the main idea in the second paragraph on this page. In your own words, explain the main idea of this paragraph.

_____
_____
_____

Comprehension Check

Underline the two main kinds of decomposers. In what kinds of places does a fungus grow?

_____
_____
_____

Some consumers are also decomposers. Decomposers break down dead plants and animals. The dead plants and animals are changed into nutrients, which go back into the soil. Producers—plants—consume these nutrients. Decomposers are very important in the ecosystem because plants need nutrients to grow.

The two main kinds of decomposers are bacteria and fungi. Bacteria are very small living things. We cannot see bacteria, but they live in soil, air, and water and on other organisms. A fungus is a plantlike organism without leaves that grows in dark, warm, wet places. Mushrooms are one kind of fungus.

Name _____   Date _____

Food Chains

The movement of food through a community is called a food chain. A food chain always begins with producers—plants. In the ocean, a food chain begins with algae, which are very small plantlike organisms. Small fish eat the algae. Medium-size-fish eat the small fish. Big fish eat the medium-size-fish.

On land, a food chain is similar. It begins with a plant. A consumer, such as an insect, eats the plant. Then another consumer, such as a bat, eats the insect. Next, a bigger consumer, such as an owl, eats the bat. Finally, the owl dies, and decomposers break it down into nutrients.

Every part of the food chain is necessary to every other part. Without water, plants die. Without plants, animals cannot live.

Choose one and complete:
1. Research the different kinds of living creatures that might live in a forest. Then make a drawing of that community.
2. Research an animal mentioned in this article. Learn more about its habitat and where it fits on the food chain. Write a short report that shows all you have learned.
3. Write a poem describing your own ecosystem. Try to include plants and animals that live in your area.

Unit 1 • Reading 2

Reading Strategy: Preview

Circle the heading of this section. Based on the heading, what do you think the section will be about?

_____
_____
_____

Text Structure

Science articles often introduce key terms in context. Underline the definition of a food chain in the first paragraph. List the links of a food chain in the ocean.

1. _____
2. _____
3. _____
4. _____

Comprehension Check

Underline the text that describes the very end of a food chain on land. How does the biggest consumer, such as an owl, contribute to the food chain?

_____
_____
_____

READING WRAP-UP

Retell It!
Think about the different parts of the food chain that feeds you. Tell the story of how this food chain works. Make sure you include how producers and small consumers make a difference to you and why they are needed.

Reader's Response
Since plants produce oxygen and humans need oxygen to breathe, it's important to protect the forests. How can you help protect the world's forests?

Think About the Skill
How did previewing the different sections help you better understand the article?

Name _____ Date _____

EDIT FOR MEANING

Read

You have read "Ecosystems: The Systems of Nature." Now read one paragraph from it again.

Habitats

Different organisms live in different habitats because they have different requirements for survival. For example, a river or lake can be the habitat of some species of freshwater fish, such as trout. Freshwater trout cannot survive in the ocean, which contains salt water. An ocean and a lake are very different habitats. Similarly, the desert in the southwestern United States and northern Mexico is the habitat of the saguaro cactus. The saguaro cactus cannot survive in a tropical rain forest.

The paragraphs below and on the next page contain the same information as the paragraph you just read. However, each contains one error. First, find the error. Then fix it by editing the sentence so that the information is correct. The first one has been done for you.

Example:

Habitats

Different organisms live in different habitats. That is because they have different needs for survival. A river or lake can be a good habitat for some species of freshwater fish, such as trout. Freshwater trout cannot survive in the ocean, which contains salt water. <u>An ocean and a freshwater lake are very ~~similar~~ *different* habitats.</u> The saguaro cactus's habitat is in the southwestern United States and northern Mexico. The saguaro cactus cannot survive in a tropical rain forest.

Unit 1 • Reading 2

Fix the Error

1. Find and fix the error.

> ### Habitats
>
> Every organism on earth can survive in any habitat. For example, some species of freshwater fish, such as trout, have a river or lake for their habitat. Freshwater trout cannot live in the sea, because it contains salt water. An ocean and a lake are different habitats. Similarly, a desert in the southwestern United States and northern Mexico is the habitat of the saguaro cactus. The saguaro cactus cannot endure life in a tropical rain forest.

2. Find and fix the error.

> ### Habitats
>
> Different organisms live in different habitats because they have different needs. For example, some species of freshwater fish, such as trout, use a river or lake as their habitat. Freshwater trout can't survive in the salt water of the ocean. A lake and an ocean are very different habitats. The tropical rain forest in Costa Rica is the habitat of the saguaro cactus.

Name _____ Date _____

FOCUS ON DETAILS

Word Search Puzzle

To complete this word search puzzle, you'll need to remember or search for details in the reading. Look at the clues and circle the answers in the puzzle below. Check off each answer. Write the word on the line next to its clue. The first answer is done for you.

1. ✓ A gas that plants produce _____oxygen_____
2. ☐ A butterfly that travels from Canada and the United States to Mexico _____
3. ☐ One kind of fungus _____
4. ☐ A carnivore that eats dead organisms _____
5. ☐ The process plants use to make food _____
6. ☐ A freshwater fish _____
7. ☐ A gas that people and animals breathe out _____
8. ☐ The ocean food chain begins with it _____
9. ☐ A decomposer we can't see _____
10. ☐ A large herbivore with four legs that people can ride _____

```
S O A Y O T W O A L E E P E C
X I M U S H R O O M Q S H D A
B Z O X Y G E N J R Q R O O R
Q A N S X Y T Y U W B N T E B
S C A V E N G E R O H S O G O
S T R O U T N V J H O R S E N
I L C G E E N K B V A Z Y D D
B R H R V R U Y N R R H N W I
I A H A R E I G S E C G T I O
Y E C C D J O A N O H J H P X
F S A T L N Q A A L G A E K I
V P R G E M B E A Q L O S Y D
L L U M L R R N C D V R I R E
E X D W F A I X O I D V S P K
M F Y Y M W I A N L U H N X B
```

Unit 1 • Reading 2

11

READ FOR FLUENCY

1. Silently read the text below. Make sure you understand the point that each sentence is making.

2. Underline the word or words in each sentence that are most important. When you read, you should say these underlined words with expression.

3. Look again at the punctuation in the paragraphs. Remember that when a sentence ends in a period, you should read the words as a statement and take a breath before beginning a new sentence. When you see a comma, you should pause briefly. When you see an exclamation mark, you should sound excited. When you see a question mark, you should read as though you are asking a question.

4. Now read the paragraphs below out loud. Pay attention to the important words and punctuation as you read.

5. Write down any words that slowed you down. Practice saying these words out loud.

6. Read the text below out loud two more times. You may want to ask a friend or family member to listen to you and tell you their reactions to your reading.

Food Chains

The movement of food through a community is called a food chain. A food chain always begins with producers—plants. In the ocean, a food chain begins with algae, which are very small plantlike organisms. Small fish eat the algae. Medium-size fish eat the small fish. Big fish eat the medium-size fish.

On land, a food chain is similar. It begins with a plant. A consumer, such as an insect, eats the plant. Then another consumer, such as a bat, eats the insect. Next, a bigger consumer, such as an owl, eats the bat. Finally, the owl dies, and decomposers break it down into nutrients.

Every part of the food chain is necessary to every other part. Without water, plants die. Without plants, animals cannot live.

Name _____ Date _____

UNIT 1: How does the natural world affect us?

READING 4: "Water and Living Things"

SUMMARY *Use with textbook pages 50–53.*

Water is very important to all living things. This passage explains how plants and animals, including people, use water. It gives information about different kinds of water found on Earth and the forms these kinds of water take. It also explains the water cycle. This natural movement of water from one place to another keeps our water fresh. Finally, it describes a Chinese government plan to deliver fresh water to areas that need it.

Visual Summary

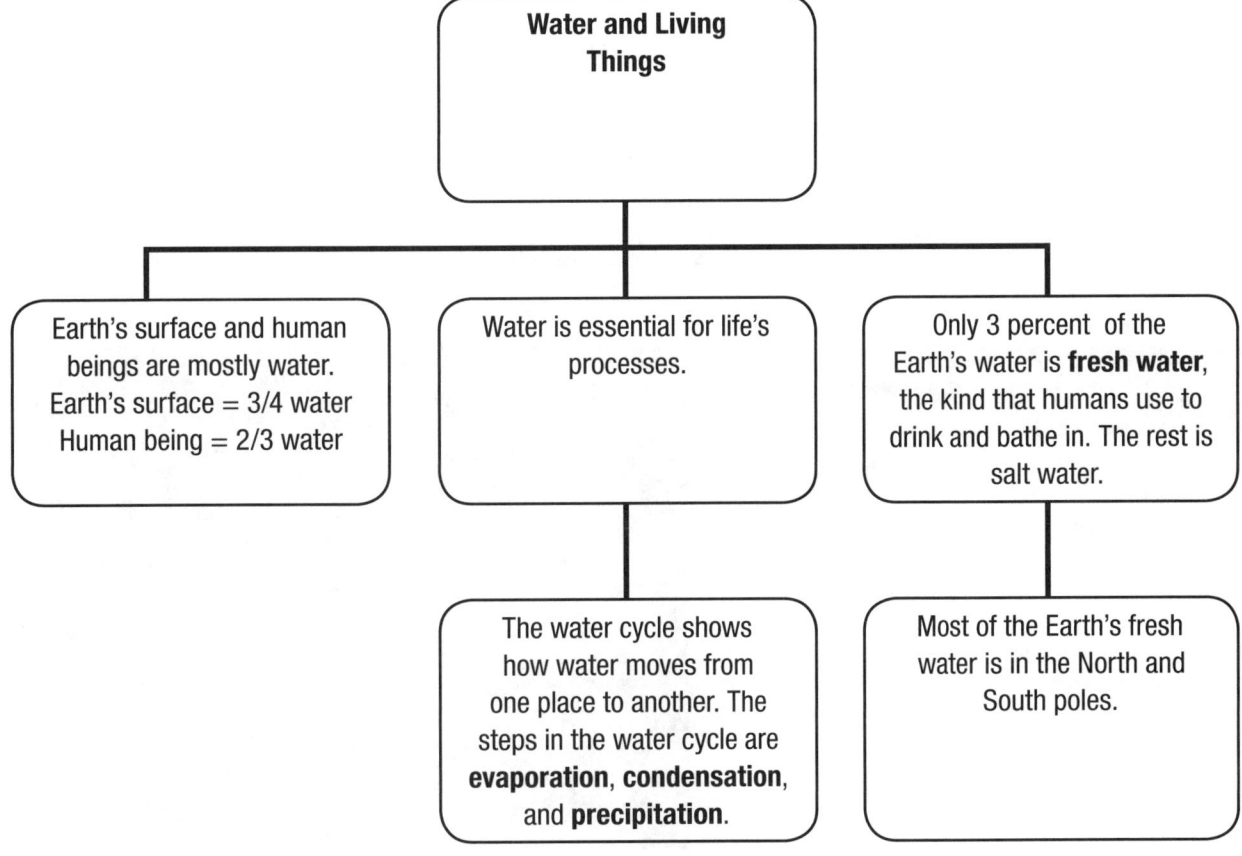

Unit 1 • Reading 4   13

Use What You Know

List three important ways that people use water every day.

1. _____
2. _____
3. _____

Text Structure

A science article often provides amounts or numbers that support a fact. Read the first paragraph on this page. Underline the facts that mention amounts or numbers. In your own words, write the most interesting fact you have just read.

_____
_____
_____

Reading Strategy: Identify Main Idea and Details

The main idea is the most important message of the paragraph. Read the second paragraph. Underline the sentence that contains the main idea. Then list two details in the paragraph that support the main idea.

1. _____
2. _____

Water and Living Things

What do Earth's surface and human beings have in common? Answer: They both consist mostly of water. Water covers about three-quarters of Earth's surface. Water makes up about two-thirds of the human body. In fact, water is a large part of *every* living thing.

Water is essential for living things to grow, reproduce, and carry out other important life processes. For example, plants use water, plus carbon dioxide and sunlight, to make their food in the process of photosynthesis. Animals and other organisms eat plants or eat other organisms that eat plants. Water is also essential as an environment for living things. Both fresh water and salt water provide habitats for many kinds of living things.

---

human beings, people
carry out, complete

14   Unit 1 • Reading 4

Name _____ Date _____

Water on Earth

Although Earth has lots of water, the amount of water that humans can use is very small. About 97 percent of Earth's water is the salt water found in the ocean. People have named different parts of the ocean, but in fact these parts are all connected, so they really form a single world ocean.

Only about 3 percent of Earth's water is fresh water. Most of that fresh water is found in the huge masses of ice near the North and South poles. Less than 1 percent of the water on Earth is available for humans to use. Some of this available fresh water is found in lakes, rivers, and streams. Other fresh water is located under the ground. This underground water is called groundwater. It fills the small cracks and spaces between underground soil and rocks.

_____

masses, amounts

Comprehension Check

Underline what the first paragraph says about the amount of water that humans can use. What kind of water do humans need?

_____
_____

Text Structure

A science textbook often has highlighted words. Their definitions are at the bottom of the page. Circle the highlighted word on this page. Look at its definition. Reread the sentence in which it appears. Rewrite the sentence without using the word.

_____
_____
_____

Comprehension Check

Underline the words in the second paragraph that explain where most fresh water is found. Why do you think most of this water cannot be used?

_____
_____
_____

Unit 1 • Reading 4

Reading Strategy: Identify Main Idea and Details

What is the main idea of the first paragraph? Underline the sentence that contains the main idea about the water cycle. List three places water in the atmosphere comes from.

1. _____
2. _____
3. _____

Text Structure

A science article often defines key terms within the text and provides examples. Underline the sentence that defines what precipitation is. List three forms of precipitation.

1. _____
2. _____
3. _____

Comprehension Check

Underline the words that describe what happens when water rises into the air. In your own words, write what happens next.

_____
_____
_____

The Water Cycle

Water is always moving from one place to another. The continuous process by which water moves through the living and nonliving parts of the environment is called the water cycle. In the water cycle, water moves from bodies of water (such as oceans, rivers, lakes, and streams), land, and living things on Earth's surface to the atmosphere and back to Earth's surface.

The sun is the source of energy that creates the water cycle. The sun's energy warms water in oceans, rivers, and lakes. Some of this water evaporates—changes into a gas called water vapor. Smaller amounts of water evaporate from the soil, from plants, and from animals (through their skin or breath). Water vapor rises in the air and forms clouds. As water vapor cools in the clouds, it condenses, or changes into liquid water drops. When water drops in the clouds become heavy, they fall back to Earth as precipitation—rain, snow, sleet, or hail.

Precipitation is the source of all fresh water on or under Earth's surface. The water cycle renews the supply of usable fresh water on Earth.

---

continuous, without stopping
clouds, tiny drops of water that collect in the air
usable, able to be used

Choose one and complete:
1. Draw a poster that encourages people not to waste water and explains why.
2. Make a list of the world's oceans. Use an atlas or a reliable online source to help you.
3. Write a letter to a friend or relative. Explain why fresh water is important.

Case Study

China's Water Challenge

China has serious environmental problems. It has recently built many factories in an effort to become an industrial power. This rapid industrial growth, along with changes in Earth's climate, have led to polluted air and rivers. Drought has made the problems even worse. China is struggling to fix these problems.

The South-North Water Diversion Plan is one possible solution. It will transfer water from the Yangtze River basin in the south of China to the very dry north, where the capital Beijing is located. The plan involves building hundreds of miles of canals. These will have to move water uphill, under the Yellow River, and through mountains. Once completed, it will be the world's largest water project.

This project will cost billions of dollars. Large areas of land will need to be flooded to create reservoirs. Over 300,000 people who live on the land will be forced to move and settle in other areas.

Some critics believe that this project is a waste of money. Water pipes often leak, and 40 percent of the water could be lost. It could also increase water pollution. But the Chinese government is determined to move forward with this project.

drought, a time when no rain falls and the land becomes very dry
diversion, change in direction
canals, long, narrow waterways
reservoirs, places where a lot of water is stored

Comprehension Check

Underline the main point the first paragraph makes about China's environmental problems. What are two reasons for China's polluted air and rivers?

_____
_____
_____

Text Structure

A science textbook often has highlighted words. Their definitions are at the bottom of the page. Circle the highlighted words in this text. Look at their definitions. Choose one of the words and write a definition for it in your own words.

_____
_____
_____

Comprehension Check

Underline what the second paragraph says about the purpose of the South-North Water Diversion Plan. What will this plan achieve?

_____
_____
_____

Unit 1 • Reading 4

READING WRAP-UP

Retell It!
Suppose you are a rain drop falling from a cloud down to Earth during a rainstorm. Tell all the things that happen to you as you travel through the water cycle. Be sure to include each stage of the water cycle in your story.

_____
_____
_____
_____
_____
_____
_____
_____
_____

Reader's Response
Since only 3 percent of the Earth's water is fresh water, it is important not to waste water. What are some ways that you can save, or conserve, water?

_____
_____
_____
_____
_____

Think About the Skill
How did finding the main idea and details of some paragraphs help you better understand the article?

_____
_____
_____
_____

Name _____ Date _____

EDIT FOR MEANING

Read
You have read "Water and Living Things." Now read one paragraph from it again.

Water and Living Things

Water is essential for living things to grow, reproduce, and carry out other important life processes. For example, plants use water, plus carbon dioxide and sunlight, to make their food in the process of photosynthesis. Animals and other organisms eat plants or eat other organisms that eat plants. Water is also essential as an environment for living things. Both fresh water and salt water provide habitats for many kinds of living things.

Unit 1 • Reading 4

Fix the Error

Each paragraph below contains the same information as the paragraph you just read. However, each paragraph contains one error. First, find the error. Then fix it by editing the sentence so that the information is correct.

1. Find and fix the error.

> ### Water and Living Things
>
> Water is a necessary ingredient for living things to grow, reproduce, and carry out other important life processes. Plants use water, plus carbon dioxide and sunlight, in the process of photosynthesis. This process makes food for the plant. No animals and organisms eat plants. Animals and organisms eat other organisms that eat plants. Water also serves as an environment for living things. Some animals and plants can live in fresh water. Some live in salt water.

2. Find and fix the error.

> ### Water and Living Things
>
> Water helps living things to grow, reproduce, and perform other important life processes. For example, plants use water, plus carbon dioxide and sunlight, to make food. This process is called photosynthesis. Animals get all their food from eating plants. Water is also a habitat for certain animals and organisms. Many living things live in either salt or fresh water.

Name _____ Date _____

FOCUS ON DETAILS

Crossword Puzzle

To complete this crossword puzzle, you'll need to remember or search for details in the reading. Use the words in the word box to help you. Not all of the words in the word box are in the puzzle. Fill in the crossword with answers to the clues below. The first answer is done for you.

Word box:
- SALTY
- WATER VAPOR
- POLES
- OCEAN
- THREE-FOURTHS
- FRESH
- ~~REPRODUCING~~
- RIVER
- EVAPORATE
- CONDENSES
- HABITAT
- TWO-THIRDS
- FOOD

Across

5. Producing a new member of a species
6. Most of the Earth's fresh water can be found here
7. Three percent of Earth's water
9. Water makes up this much of human bodies

Down

1. Water as a gas
2. Plants turn water, sunlight, and carbon dioxide into this
3. The largest body of water
4. When water changes from gas to small drops, it does this
8. The area in which animals live

Unit 1 • Reading 4

READ FOR FLUENCY

1. Silently read the text below. Make sure you understand the point that each sentence is making.

2. Underline the word or words in each sentence that are most important. When you read, you should say these underlined words with expression.

3. Look again at the punctuation in the paragraphs. Remember that when a sentence ends in a period, you should read the words as a statement and take a breath before beginning a new sentence. When you see a comma, you should pause briefly. When you see an exclamation mark, you should sound excited. When you see a question mark, you should read as though you are asking a question.

4. Now read the paragraphs below out loud. Pay attention to the important words and punctuation as you read.

5. Write down any words that slowed you down. Practice saying these words out loud.

6. Read the text below out loud two more times. You may want to ask a friend or family member to listen to you and tell you their reactions to your reading.

The Water Cycle

Water is always moving from one place to another. The continuous process by which water moves through the living and nonliving parts of the environment is called the water cycle. In the water cycle, water moves from bodies of water (such as oceans, rivers, lakes, and streams), land, and living things on Earth's surface to the atmosphere and back to Earth's surface.

The sun is the source of energy that creates the water cycle. The sun's energy warms water in oceans, rivers, and lakes. Some of this water evaporates—changes into a gas called water vapor. Smaller amounts of water evaporate from the soil, from plants, and from animals (through their skin or breath). Water vapor rises in the air and forms clouds. As water vapor cools in the clouds, it condenses, or changes into liquid water drops. When water drops in the clouds become heavy, they fall back to Earth as precipitation—rain, snow, sleet, or hail.

Name _____ Date _____

 **Where can a journey take you?**

READING 2: "Early Explorers"

SUMMARY *Use with textbook pages 86–89.*

This passage tells about early traders and explorers from around 700 B.C.E. to the early 1500s. First it tells about the Phoenicians. They sailed the Mediterranean Sea, trading goods and setting up new colonies. Next, it tells about the Vikings. They invaded Europe and traveled far across the Atlantic Ocean. After that, it tells how explorers developed land and sea trade routes between Europe and Asia. This led to Christopher Columbus's voyages to the Americas.

Visual Summary

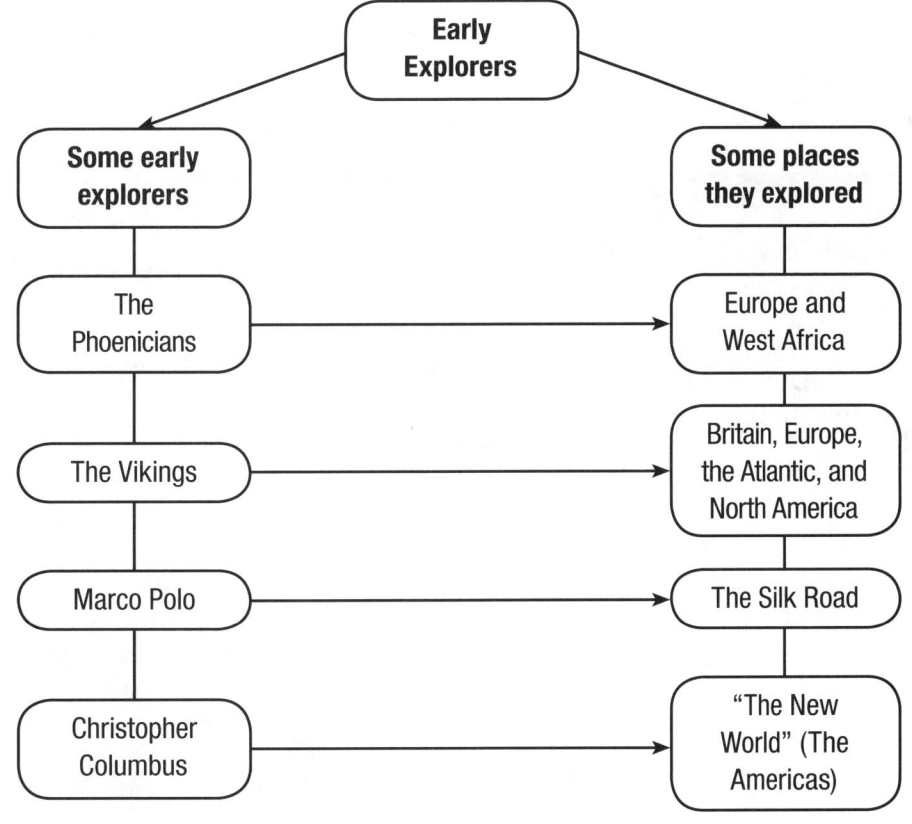

Unit 2 • Reading 2

Use What You Know

Describe something you have traded. Maybe you exchanged money for something you wanted, or traded one item for another.

_____
_____
_____

Text Structure

A social studies article contains information about dates and places. Underline the date when Phoenicians first began trading. Then write down two places where they explored.

Mark the Text

_____
_____

Reading Strategy: Using Visuals

Remember that visuals can be photographs, illustrations, maps, charts, and graphic organizers. What does this photograph of a silver coin show you about the Phoenicians?

_____
_____
_____
_____

Early Explorers

The Phoenicians

Six thousand years ago people grew their own food and made everything they needed. They did not travel far. They did not know what lay beyond a few days' journey from their homes.

However, as civilizations developed, people saw and wanted new products. So the idea of trading goods evolved. One of the earliest peoples to begin trading were the Phoenicians. They lived on the Mediterranean coast of modern-day Israel and Lebanon. The Phoenicians were expert shipbuilders, able to sail great distances. They understood that they could make money by trading.

Between about 700 B.C.E. and 100 B.C.E., Phoenician ships explored the lands that border the Mediterranean Sea. They searched for new markets. They established colonies. They even sailed through the Strait of Gibraltar to the Atlantic, reaching Britain and West Africa.

---

evolved, developed slowly

24　　　　　　　　　　　　　　　　　　　　　Unit 2 • Reading 2

Name _____ Date _____

Viking Voyages

The Vikings were from Scandinavia, a region in northern Europe. From the eighth to the twelfth century, Vikings built magnificent sailing vessels and set out from their homeland on voyages of exploration.

During the early Middle Ages, Viking raiders invaded many other parts of Europe. The reasons for these journeys were varied. Some Vikings were interested only in stealing treasure and capturing slaves. They plundered the unlucky communities they found in Britain and the Mediterranean. Other Vikings were in search of new lands across the Atlantic. Viking farmers needed new places to settle, as farmland in Scandinavia was scarce and poor. The Swedish Vikings set their sights on the lands of Eastern Europe and Asia. Mainly traders, these Vikings hoped to develop new markets for exchanging goods. By 1000, the Vikings had also reached North America.

After about 1200, the Vikings became more settled. Their long voyages of discovery ceased.

---

voyages, long trips
plundered, stole money or property
scarce, not enough
ceased, stopped

Comprehension Check

Underline the section of the text that states where the Vikings were from. Can you infer that the Vikings lived near a large body of water? Why or why not?

_____
_____
_____

Text Structure

Social studies articles explain how and why events took place. Underline the sentence that explains why the Vikings plundered other lands. List two areas the Vikings plundered.

1. _____

2. _____

Comprehension Check

Circle the time period when the Vikings became more settled. Why do you think the Vikings stopped plundering other lands?

_____
_____
_____

Unit 2 • Reading 2

Text Structure

Social studies articles often explain facts and figures. Underline the figure that describes the length of the Silk Road. List two geographical features that the Silk Road crossed.

1. _____

2. _____

Comprehension Check

Underline the sentence that states the most important product traded along the Silk Road. Why do you think this was such an important product?

_____
_____
_____

Reading Strategy: Use Visuals

When you study the visuals along with the text, it is easier to understand the meaning of the text. Study the map. Which two routes does the map show?

1. _____

2. _____

The Silk Road

Not all exploration took place over rolling seas. The Silk Road was a land route between Europe and Asia. It was used from around 500 B.C.E. until sea routes to China were opened up in about 1650. The most important product traded along the Silk Road was silk. For centuries the Chinese kept the secret of how to make silk from other nations.

Along this road, trade was conducted between China and Europe. Chinese merchants sent silk and spices to Europe over the mountains and deserts of Asia. In return, gold, silver, and horses were imported to China. The road was about 7,000 kilometers (4,300 mi.) long and very dangerous.

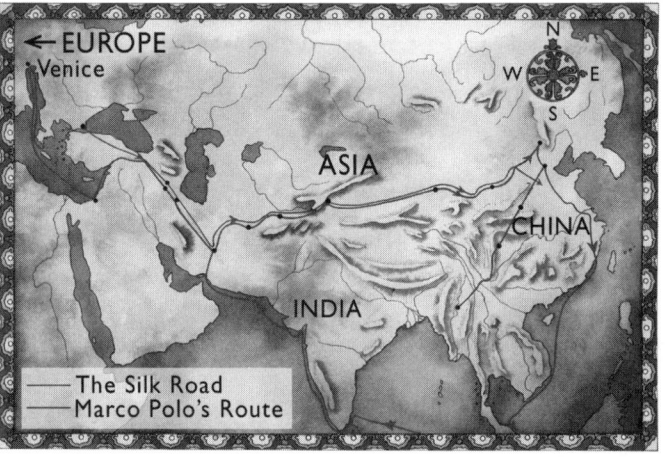

It passed through numerous kingdoms where rulers demanded gifts from travelers. In addition, bandits would often pillage a traveling camel train. Because of these dangers, the goods were passed from one merchant to another, with no trader traveling for more than a few hundred miles at a time.

Marco Polo was a trader and great storyteller from Venice, Italy. He was the first European explorer to travel the entire length of the Silk Road in the thirteenth century. It took him four years, and he wrote about his travels. The Silk Road became less important after European ships began a regular trade with China around the southern tip of Africa.

The Age of Exploration

The Age of Exploration began in fifteenth-century Portugal. In 1415, Prince Henry of Portugal, known as Henry the Navigator, took command of a port in northern Morocco. Henry sent out his ships to explore the west coast of Africa. He paid for many expeditions that eventually reached Sierra Leone on Africa's west coast. Later kings of Portugal financed expeditions that sailed around the Cape of Good Hope at the southern tip of Africa. This opened up trade routes to India, China, and the Indonesian and Philippine Islands (called the Spice Islands). Portugal became rich and powerful through its control of trade in this area.

---

bandits, people who rob or attack
pillage, steal things using violence, especially during war

Comprehension Check

Underline the section of text that describes why goods were passed from one merchant to the next. Why do you think passing goods between merchants was necessary?

Text Structure

Social studies articles often provide details about individuals who were involved in historic events. Circle three details that describe Marco Polo. What evidence from the text indicates that Marco Polo was persistent?

Comprehension Check

Underline the sections of the text that describe the areas of Africa that Henry the Navigator commanded and explored. Why do you think control of these areas made Portugal rich and powerful?

Unit 2 • Reading 2

Comprehension Check

Underline the section of text that describes how much knowledge most Europeans had of the world outside Europe. Why do you suppose Europeans in the 1400s had this amount of knowledge about the rest of the world?

_____

_____

_____

Text Structure

Social studies articles often contain concrete examples. Underline the section of text that describes stories that amazed Europeans. Why do you think the Europeans often didn't believe that the stories were true?

_____

_____

_____

Comprehension Check

Underline the name of the Italian navigator who calculated the distance to the East Indies. What detail from the text suggests that the navigator didn't think the distance was very far?

_____

_____

_____

The New World

In the late fifteenth century even the most educated Europeans knew little about the world outside Europe. The stories travelers brought back were so amazing that few people believed them. Thick jungles stretched south of the Sahara Desert. To the west lay the vast Atlantic Ocean. Nobody knew how wide the Atlantic was, nor what lay on the other side.

Then, in 1480, Italian navigator Christopher Columbus announced that, by his calculations, the East Indies lay only 4,500 kilometers (2,795 mi.) to the west.

---

calculations, ways of using numbers to find an answer

Few experts agreed with him. Indeed, he was later proved wrong. Nevertheless, the Spanish king and queen paid for his expedition. Columbus landed on islands in the Caribbean Sea. People called the Tainos were living on these islands. Columbus thought he had landed in India, so he called the Tainos *Indians*. When Columbus returned to Spain, he brought back gold, pearls, parrots, and some Taino people.

The Spanish made the islands a colony, and the Tainos became slaves. The Spanish brought diseases to the islands, and many Taino people died.

This voyage to the Americas was one of the most important that took place during the Age of Exploration. It opened up the New World to Europe.

Choose one and complete:

1. On a long strip of paper, make a timeline that tells about the Age of Exploration. Use the information from the text for dates and names. Be sure to put the events in order. Illustrate your timeline.
2. Draw and label a picture of some of the goods European traders brought back from China. Make a second drawing of the goods the Chinese people received in exchange. Write a short paragraph about how the trading might have helped both groups of people.
3. Write a poem about the Taino people. Remember that a poem does not have to use rhyming words. Try to develop clear images and to use fresh language in your poem.

Comprehension Check

Underline what the article says about who paid for Columbus's expedition. Why do you think these people paid for the expedition?

_____
_____
_____

Text Structure

Social studies articles often describe the conditions in which human beings live. Underline what the text says about the changes the Taino people faced because of Columbus's discovery. Did the Taino people benefit from the changes? Why or why not?

_____
_____
_____

Reading Strategy: Use Visuals

Study the illustration of Columbus on page 28. List a detail from the illustration that gives you new information about Columbus's expedition.

_____
_____

Unit 2 • Reading 2

READING WRAP-UP

Retell It!
Pretend you are a sailor on Christopher Columbus's voyage to the Americas. Tell about the voyage in your own words.

_____
_____
_____
_____
_____
_____
_____
_____

Reader's Response
If you were the king or queen of Spain at the time of Columbus's expedition, would you have colonized the islands of the Caribbean? Why or why not?

_____
_____
_____
_____
_____

Think About the Skill
How did using the visuals help you to better understand what you were reading?

_____
_____
_____
_____

EDIT for MEANING

Read

You have read "Early Explorers." Now read one paragraph from it again.

The Age of Exploration

The Age of Exploration began in fifteenth-century Portugal. In 1415, Prince Henry of Portugal, known as Henry the Navigator, took command of a port in northern Morocco. Henry sent out his ships to explore the west coast of Africa. He paid for many expeditions that eventually reached Sierra Leone on Africa's west coast. Later kings of Portugal financed expeditions that sailed around the Cape of Good Hope at the southern tip of Africa.

Fix the Error

Each paragraph below contains the same information as the paragraph you just read. However, each paragraph contains one error. First, find the error. Then fix it by editing the sentence so that the information is correct.

1. Find and fix the error.

The Age of Exploration

In Portugal, in the 1400s, the period known as the Age of Exploration began. Prince Henry of Portugal seized command of a port in northern Morocco in 1415. He became known as Henry the Navigator. Henry did not allow his ships to explore the west coast of Africa. It was Prince Henry's money that financed many expeditions that ultimately reached Sierra Leone on Africa's west coast. Later Portuguese kings would pay for expeditions around the southern tip of Africa, called the Cape of Good Hope.

---

2. Find and fix the error.

The Age of Exploration

The fifteenth century is known as the Age of Exploration. It started in Portugal where in 1415, a young prince became known as Henry the Navigator. In 1415, Henry took command of a port in northern Morocco. He ordered ships to explore the west coast of Africa. Although he paid for many expeditions, they never accomplished anything or went anywhere new. In later years, the kings of Portugal would fund voyages around the Cape of Good Hope, at the southern tip of Africa.

Name _____ Date _____

FOCUS ON DETAILS

Mystery Word Puzzle

To complete this mystery word puzzle, you'll need to remember or search for details in the reading. Use the clues to help you unscramble each of the words. Write the words in the boxes. The first answer is done for you. The numbered letters will form the mystery word.

1. Exchanging goods with other people

    DRTAGIN | T | R | A | D | I | N | G |
                        4

2. The earliest traders

    NICSNAIPHEO | | | | | | | | | | |
                            2

3. Explorers from Scandinavia

    KIVNGSI | | | | | | | |
                    1

4. The reason Vikings searched for new lands

    NIGMAFR | | | | | | | |

5. A land route between Europe and Asia

    KSLI AODR | | | | | | | | |

6. The first European trader to travel the entire Silk Road

    OCRMA LOOP | | | | | | | | | |

7. The prince in Portugal who financed many explorations

    RYENH | | | | | |
                      3

8. The most southern tip of Africa

    EPCA FO DOOG HPEO | | | | | | | | | | | |
                                6   5

What is the name for a long trip across water?

| | | | A | | |
  1   2   3   4   5   6

Unit 2 • Reading 2   33

READ for FLUENCY

1. Silently read the text below. Make sure you understand the point that each sentence is making.

2. Underline the word or words in each sentence that are most important. When you read, you should say these underlined words with expression.

3. Look again at the punctuation in the paragraphs. Remember that when a sentence ends in a period, you should read the words as a statement and take a breath before beginning a new sentence. When you see a comma, you should pause briefly. When you see an exclamation mark, you should sound excited. When you see a question mark, you should read as though you are asking a question.

4. Now read the paragraphs below out loud. Pay attention to the important words and punctuation as you read.

5. Write down any words that slowed you down. Practice saying these words out loud.

6. Read the text below out loud two more times. You may want to ask a friend or family member to listen to you and tell you their reactions to your reading.

Viking Voyages

The Vikings were from Scandinavia, a region in northern Europe. From the eighth to the twelfth century, Vikings built magnificent sailing vessels and set out from their homeland on voyages of exploration.

During the early Middle Ages, Viking raiders invaded many other parts of Europe. The reasons for these journeys were varied. Some Vikings were interested only in stealing treasure and capturing slaves. They plundered the unlucky communities they found in Britain and the Mediterranean. Other Vikings were in search of new lands across the Atlantic. Viking farmers needed new places to settle, as farmland in Scandinavia was scarce and poor. The Swedish Vikings set their sights on the lands of Eastern Europe and Asia. Mainly traders, these Vikings hoped to develop new markets for exchanging goods. By 1000, the Vikings had also reached North America.

Name _____ Date _____

Where can a journey take you?

READING 3: "Migrating Caribou" and "Magnets in Animals"

SUMMARY Use with textbook pages 98–101.

The first passage tells about a kind of deer called caribou. It explains how they migrate, or move from one place to another. In summer, caribou live in grassy areas near the Arctic Circle called the tundra. When the weather gets colder, they get together in large groups called herds. They travel hundreds of miles south to spend winter in the forests. In the spring, they move north again, as far as the North Pole. There the female caribou give birth to their babies. At the start of summer, the animals again travel south to the grassy tundra. This completes their migration cycle. The second passage gives facts about the migration routes of different animals. It suggests how animals find their way. Scientists think they use the sun, stars, or landmarks. They also think some animals might have a kind of magnetic compass inside their bodies.

Visual Summary

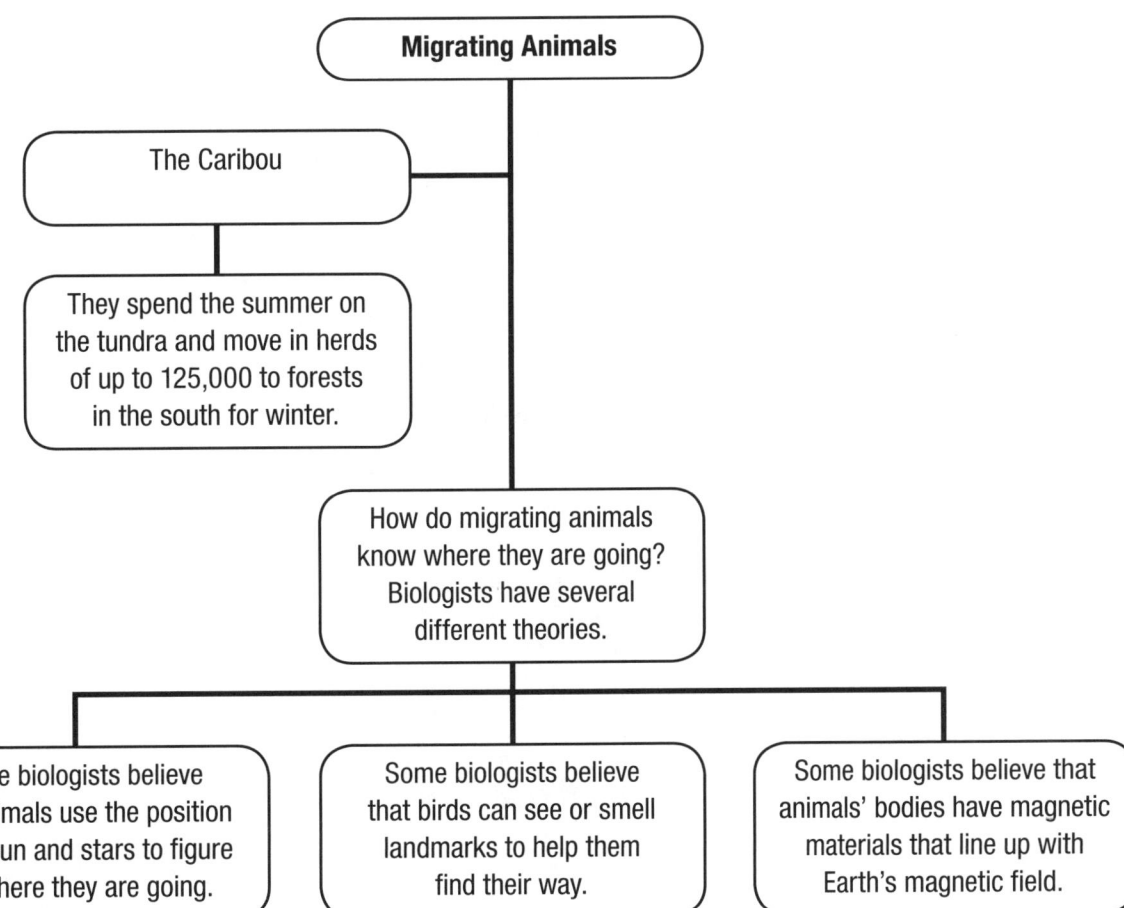

Unit 2 • Reading 3   35

Use What You Know

List two things you know about the coldest areas on Earth.

1. _____

2. _____

Text Structure

Science articles present factual information to readers. They also present explanations for the facts. Underline an important fact in paragraph 1 of the text. Then write an explanation for the fact below.

_____
_____
_____
_____

Reading Strategy: Recognize Cause and Effect

A cause is a reason something happens; an effect is the result of what happens. Underline the cause for the caribou migration from the frozen north to the forest in the south. Why do you think the caribou follow the same migration patterns as their ancestors?

_____
_____
_____

Migrating Caribou

Migrating Caribou

If you fly over the Arctic in the fall, you will see an amazing sight: thousands of migrating caribou flowing across the landscape like a thin, brown river. They are traveling from the frozen north of the Arctic to the forest in the south. They are going to a warmer place in search of food.

Caribou are members of the deer family. They stand about 1½ meters (4–5 ft.) tall from the ground to their shoulders and have small ears and tails. These caribou are barren-ground caribou. *Barren ground* means "lacking plants or crops." These words perfectly describe the land of the Arctic tundra, the cold, treeless regions of northern Asia, Europe, and North America where these caribou live. In these harsh lands, several million barren-ground caribou follow the same migration patterns their ancestors did thousands of years ago.

Barren-ground caribou are social animals. They travel in large herds made up of thousands. Caribou eat grass, mushrooms, twigs, and shrubs, but their favorite food is lichen. Lichen is a low-growing plant that is common in the Arctic. It grows on rocks and trees. One caribou can eat four kilograms (9 lb.) of lichen a day.

---

harsh, very uncomfortable
ancestors, family members from the past

Name _____ Date _____

The caribou spend the summer in the northern part of their range. There, they reproduce (have babies) and move from pasture to pasture. On the summer range, the new calves grow healthy and fat. However, the tundra is a harsh and windy place during the long winter. Deep, wind-hardened snow covers the ground. The caribou cannot scrape through the thick ice to reach the food they need. A big snowfall or a rapid drop in temperature inspires the caribou to move south to avoid starvation.

Caribou cover about 20 to 65 kilometers (12–40 mi.) a day while migrating. They are excellent swimmers and can easily cross wide lakes and rivers. Different caribou herds migrate different distances. Large herds usually travel longer distances. The Porcupine caribou herd contains about 125,000 animals. It travels about 650 kilometers (400 mi.). The Central Arctic herd contains about 25,000 animals and migrates about 200 kilometers (125 mi.). However, the herds actually travel much more than this. They wander back and forth, adding many kilometers to their journeys.

range, area of land
inspires, encourages

Comprehension Check
Underline the section of text that describes the part of the range where caribou spend the summer. Why do you think they spend the summer there?

_____
_____
_____

Reading Strategy: Recognize Cause and Effect
Underline what the text explains as the reason why the caribou migrate south. If the effect is the caribou moving south, what is the cause?

_____
_____
_____

Text Structure
Science articles often include number facts to help explain certain events. Circle two number facts in the text. Describe what these number facts help you to understand.

_____
_____
_____

Unit 2 • Reading 3

Reading Strategy: Recognize Cause and Effect

Underline what the first paragraph says about the snow and lichen south of the tree line.
On the first line below, write which fact is the cause. On the second line, write which fact is the effect.

1. _____
2. _____

Comprehension Check

Underline why the caribou go north to have their babies. Give one reason why the calves are safer in the north.

_____
_____
_____
_____

Text Structure

Science articles often include definitions or explanations of important words.
Underline an important word that is defined in the article. Why is this word important to this part of the article?

_____
_____
_____
_____

The caribou travel for several months. In December, they arrive at their winter range, south of the Arctic tree line, in the forest. North of the tree line, no trees will grow. South of the tree line, the snow remains soft. This makes it easier for the caribou to find lichen to eat.

In April and May, the snow begins to melt. This is a sign for pregnant female caribou, called cows, to leave. The cows begin the long migration to their calving grounds back in the northern Arctic. Why do the caribou travel so far to have their babies? In the north, the young calves are much safer. Predators like wolves and bears are less common there. The best calving grounds also have a lot of new plants, which are high-energy food. This allows the mother caribou to produce rich milk for their calves. And the cool breezes keep away mosquitoes and biting flies. For the caribou, it is worth traveling hundreds of kilometers to reach these special places.

---

predators, animals that kill and eat other animals

The caribou travel through deep snow and cross ice-filled rivers to reach their destination. After two months and about 1,000 kilometers (600 mi.) of walking, the cows finally reach the northern Arctic. The young are born in early June, almost as soon as their mothers arrive. The other caribou follow several weeks later.

The caribou stay on their summer range for one or two months. At first, they spend their time alone or in small groups. Then the herd begins to gather, and thousands of caribou start to move across the landscape. They begin their long southward journey again, away from the tundra and back across the tree line to the forest.

destination, place at the end of a journey

Comprehension Check

Underline what the article says about how different caribou arrive at different times to their northern range. Why do you suppose some caribou arrive before others?

_____
_____
_____

Reading Strategy: Recognize Cause and Effect

Read what the text says about how long it takes for the caribou to migrate north. What is the effect or result of their migration? In other words, what do the caribou do once they reach the northern range?

_____
_____
_____

Comprehension Check

Underline what the text says about how long the caribou stay on their summer range. Why do you think the caribou gather in herds when they begin their southward journey again?

_____
_____
_____

Unit 2 • Reading 3   39

Text Structure

Science articles often include definitions of important words. Underline the two words that are defined in this part of the text. On the lines below, write their definitions in your own words.

1. _____

2. _____

Reading Strategy: Recognize Cause and Effect

Read what the text says about monarch butterflies. Why do monarch butterflies fly south in winter?

_____

Comprehension Check

Underline what the text says about where animals migrate. Why do you suppose many animals migrate north for summer and south for winter?

_____

Magnets in Animals
by Darlene R. Stille

Every year, many animals migrate, or travel, from one place to another. Some animals go north for summer and south for winter. They may make round trips that cover thousands of miles. Swarms of monarch butterflies travel from Canada and the northern United States to spend the winter in places as far south as Mexico.

Some whales and fish swim across the open sea. One kind of sea turtle finds its way between South America and a tiny island in the middle of the Atlantic Ocean.

Every autumn, flocks of ducks and geese fly overhead. They travel south for the winter. Some are making a journey of thousands of miles.

---

swarms, large group of insects that move together
flocks, groups

40   Unit 2 • Reading 3

Name _____ Date _____

Arctic terns are migrating birds that cover up to 22,000 miles (35,400 kilometers) every year.

How do animals find their way? Biologists think that some animals use the position of the sun and the stars to help tell where they are going. Some animals may see or even smell landmarks to find their way.

Many biologists now think that some animals have a built-in compass. They think that certain birds, insects, fish, and other sea animals have tiny bits of magnetic material in their bodies. The tiny magnets line up along Earth's magnetic field. Somehow the animals use these compasses inside their bodies to find their way over thousands of miles.

Comprehension Check

Underline the description of how far an arctic tern migrates every year. Based on what you have read so far, what do you think are its reasons for migrating?

_____
_____
_____

Text Structure

Science articles often explain how things happen. Underline one explanation for how migrating animals are able to find their way. Then write the explanation in your own words below.

_____
_____
_____
_____

Comprehension Check

Underline what the last paragraph says about what some biologists believe is the reason for a bird's internal compass. In your own words, describe how this idea works.

_____
_____
_____
_____

Choose one and complete:

1. Select one of the migrating animals described in this reading. Make a poster that illustrates the animal and the foods it eats. Write number facts and other facts about the animal on the poster.

2. Use reliable websites to do an online search for more information about one of the migrating animals. Organize this information around causes and effects. Display your information in a cause-and-effect chart.

3. Write important facts about migrating animals on index cards. On the opposite side of each index card, write a question about why the migrating animal migrates. Play a quiz game. The person who answers the most cards correctly wins.

Unit 2 • Reading 3

READING WRAP-UP

Retell It!
Pretend you are a writer of a television program about migrating animals. Prepare an introduction to the program that explains why some animals migrate. Make your writing entertaining for a television audience.

_____
_____
_____
_____
_____
_____
_____
_____

Reader's Response
If you could spend time as a scientist observing one kind of migrating animal, which one would you choose? What interests you about this type of animal?

_____
_____
_____
_____
_____
_____

Think About the Skill
How did your understanding of the article improve when you practiced recognizing cause and effect?

_____
_____
_____
_____

Name _____ Date _____

EDIT FOR MEANING

Read

You have read "Migrating Caribou" and "Magnets in Animals." Now read one paragraph again.

> **Migrating Caribou**
>
> Why do the caribou travel so far to have their babies? In the north, the young calves are much safer. Predators like wolves and bears are less common there. The best calving grounds also have a lot of new plants, which are high-energy food. This allows the mother caribou to produce rich milk for their calves. And the cool breezes keep away mosquitoes and biting flies. For the caribou, it is worth traveling hundreds of kilometers to reach these special places.

Unit 2 • Reading 3   43

Fix the Error

Each paragraph below contains the same information as the paragraph you just read. However, each paragraph contains one error. First, find the error. Then fix it by editing the sentence so the information is correct.

1. Find and fix the error.

> **Migrating Caribou**
>
> The caribou travel a long way to have their babies. There are several reasons for this. Calves are safer in the north, because wolves, bears and other predators are less common there. Good calving grounds also have lots of new plants, which are very low-energy food. This allows the mother caribou to produce rich milk for their calves. Also, the cool winds keep away biting insects, like flies and mosquitoes. For the caribou, this long migration is definitely worth it.

2. Find and fix the error.

> **Migrating Caribou**
>
> Why do the caribou choose to have their babies so far north? First, the calves are much safer there. Predators, such as wolves and bears, are quite common in the calving grounds. The best areas also have a lot of new plants, which are high-energy food for mother caribou. This allows them to produce rich milk for their calves. The cool breezes keep flies and mosquitoes away. It is worth it for the caribou to travel a long way to reach theses special places.

FOCUS ON DETAILS

Crossword Puzzle

To complete this crossword puzzle, you'll need to remember or search for details in the reading. Use the words in the word box to help you. Not all of the words in the word box are in the puzzle. Fill in the crossword with answers to the clues below.

Word Box:
- ~~MIGRATION~~
- COMPASS
- CARIBOU
- HIGH ENERGY
- LICHEN
- MOSSES
- ARCTIC
- ARCTIC TERN
- LANDMARKS
- CIRCLE
- LOW CALORIE

Across

2. A plant that grows on rocks in the Arctic
5. An animal in the deer family that eats lichen
6. Memorable places or objects that help animals find their way
7. A bird that migrates up to 22,000 (35,400 kilometers) miles

Down

1. Movement from one region to another
3. A magnetic device that points to the North
4. A type of food pregnant caribou need

Unit 2 • Reading 3

READ FOR FLUENCY

1. Silently read the text below. Make sure you understand the point that each sentence is making.

2. Underline the word or words in each sentence that are most important. When you read, you should say these underlined words with expression.

3. Look again at the punctuation in the paragraphs. Remember that when a sentence ends in a period, you should read the words as a statement and take a breath before beginning a new sentence. When you see a comma, you should pause briefly. When you see an exclamation mark, you should sound excited. When you see a question mark, you should read as though you are asking a question.

4. Now read the paragraphs below out loud. Pay attention to the important words and punctuation as you read.

5. Write down any words that slowed you down. Practice saying these words out loud.

6. Read the text below out loud two more times. You may want to ask a friend or family member to listen to you and tell you their reactions to your reading.

Migrating Caribou

In April and May, the snow begins to melt. This is a sign for pregnant female caribou, called cows, to leave. The cows begin the long migration to their calving grounds back in the northern Arctic. Why do the caribou travel so far to have their babies? In the north, the young calves are much safer. Predators like wolves and bears are less common there. The best calving grounds also have a lot of new plants, which are high-energy food. This allows the mother caribou to produce rich milk for their calves. And the cool breezes keep away mosquitoes and biting flies. For the caribou, it is worth traveling hundreds of kilometers to reach these special places.

Name _____ Date _____

What defines success?

READING 1: "Success Stories"

SUMMARY *Use with textbook pages 136–139.*

This passage tells about four people and how they succeeded in different ways. Frida Kahlo was a Mexican painter. She overcame disease and injury to become a world-famous painter. Bill Gates created Microsoft and became the world's richest man. Then he and his wife started the Bill and Melinda Gates Foundation. It gives money to end the world's diseases. Muhammad Yunus is an economist who started a bank. It lends small amounts of money to the poorest people in Bangladesh. He and his bank won the Nobel Peace Prize in 2006. Dr. Mae Jemison became the first African-American woman to go into space. She later became the director of an institute that studies how modern technologies can help developing countries.

Visual Summary

Success Stories

Frida Kahlo	Bill Gates	Muhammad Yunus	Mae Jemison
Painter who triumphed over many obstacles, including the disease of polio, to become one of the most respected artists of her time.	Founder of Microsoft, world's richest person, and funder of malaria research and many other charities.	Economist who came up with idea to give small loans to extremely poor women in developing countries. Winner of Nobel Peace Prize.	African-American astronaut and university professor who helps create technologies that improve the lives of poor people in developing countries.

Unit 3 • Reading 1   47

Use What You Know

List three reasons why someone might decide to become an artist.

1. _____
2. _____
3. _____

Text Structure

Social studies articles often give facts about a person or event. **Mark the Text** Underline the first sentence. What did Frida Kahlo do for a living?

_____
_____
_____

Reading Strategy: Connect Ideas

When you read more than one article on a common topic, **Mark the Text** take notes to find connections between the ideas in the articles. Underline the sentence that tells what happened to Kahlo when she was in college. What connection can you make between the accident and Kahlo becoming an artist?

_____
_____
_____

Success Stories

Frida Kahlo

Born in 1907, the extraordinary painter Frida Kahlo grew up in Coyoacán, an area which is now part of Mexico City. When she was six years old, Kahlo got polio, a serious disease that often causes paralysis. As a result of her illness, Kahlo's right leg was always thinner and weaker than her left one. She was also involved in a terrible bus accident when she was in college. Her injuries were so severe she was often hospitalized. It took her many months to recover from this accident. It was during this time that Kahlo began to paint from her bed.

At the age of twenty-one, Kahlo met Diego Rivera, a very famous Mexican painter. They got married in 1929. They shared a love of Mexican art and culture. In some of her self-portraits, Kahlo is wearing traditional Mexican clothing and jewelry. In addition to her many self-portraits, Kahlo painted portraits of friends. She is also famous for her still-life paintings—pictures of arranged objects, such as flowers and fruit.

Frida Kahlo exhibited her work in New York City, Paris, and Mexico City. She died at the young age of forty-seven. Her house in Mexico City, called Casa Azul (Blue House), is now the Frida Kahlo Museum. Her work and her life story continue to impress people all over the world.

---

paralysis, the loss of the ability to move or feel part of your body
exhibited, showed in public

Name _____ Date _____

Bill Gates

As an elementary school student in Seattle, Washington, in the 1960s, Bill Gates excelled in science and mathematics. When he was in eighth grade, his school acquired an early computer. Bill Gates was excused from math class so he could work on a program for the computer. Later, he went to Harvard University, where he spent most of his time in the university's computer center.

In 1975, Bill Gates started the Microsoft Corporation. The company developed Windows, the world's most widely used computer operating system. Bill Gates eventually became a multibillionaire and the richest man in the world.

In 2000, Gates and his wife started the Bill and Melinda Gates Foundation. So far, the foundation has contributed $800 million to the United Nations Global Alliance for Vaccine and Immunization, to fight diseases. One disease, malaria, is spread by mosquitoes. Malaria affects about 500 million people every year and kills as many as 3 million people—mostly African children under five years of age. An easy way to prevent malaria is by using bed nets, which cost very little. But very few families can afford them.

Bill Gates has said: "It just blows my mind how little money has been spent on malaria research. . . . I just keep asking myself, Do we really not care because it doesn't affect us? . . . I refuse to sit there and say, Okay, next problem, this one doesn't bother me. It does bother me. Very much. And the only way for that to change is to stop malaria. So that is what we are going to have to do."

---

program, set of instructions
contributed, given; donated
blows my mind, amazes me

Unit 3 • Reading 1

Comprehension Check

Underline the sentence that tells what Bill Gates's best subjects were in elementary school. How do you think his early interests helped him start the Microsoft Corporation?

_____
_____
_____

Reading Strategy: Connect Ideas

As you take notes on articles, look for common ideas between them.
Underline the name of the most widely used computer operating system. How do you think that the development of this system led to Gates becoming the richest man in the world?

_____
_____
_____

Comprehension Check

Underline how much money the Gates Foundation gave to the United Nations to fight malaria. Why do you think the Gateses want to stop malaria?

_____
_____
_____

Text Structure

A social studies article often includes important facts about a person. Underline the sentence that tells about Muhammad Yunus's education. What did he do after he earned his doctorate?

_____

Reading Strategy: Connect Ideas

Underline the event that led Muhammad Yunus to start the Grameen Bank. How did the famine and his teaching lead Yunus to run a bank?

_____

_____

_____

Comprehension Check

Underline the word that describes the tiny loans that Yunus gives out. List three things that made his plan different from that of other banks.

1. _____
2. _____
3. _____

Muhammad Yunus

Muhammad Yunus was born in 1940 in a village in Bangladesh. He obtained a scholarship to study in the United States and earned a doctorate. He returned to Bangladesh in 1972 to teach economics.

In 1974, Bangladesh suffered a terrible famine. Yunus decided that it was not enough to teach economics and read textbooks. He needed to do something practical. What if these people were able to receive tiny loans, or microcredit, to try to improve their situation? Yunus started his project in a small village. He lent $27 to a group of forty-two villagers. They made bamboo stools and bought a cow. And so the Grameen Bank was born.

The Grameen Bank was very different from other banks. First, it provided very small loans. Second, it focused on women borrowers. Yunus believed that women were better at using and repaying loans. Third, only the very poorest people could obtain loans. The system was based on the trust of the bank and the enterprise of the women borrowers. If the borrowers failed to repay, the bank would fail. But it didn't.

In 2006, Muhammad Yunus and the Grameen Bank were awarded the Nobel Peace Prize. The Nobel committee said, "Lasting peace cannot be achieved unless large population groups find ways in which to break out of poverty. Microcredit is one such means...."

---

doctorate, university degree of the highest level
economics, the way goods and services are produced and used
practical, relating to actions, not words
borrowers, people who use something and give it back later

Mae Jemison

Mae Jemison was born in 1956 in Decatur, Alabama. She grew up in Chicago, Illinois. When she was growing up, Jemison watched spaceflights on television. After college, she went to medical school and also took graduate courses in engineering. What she really wanted, however, was to be a space traveler. In 1987, Dr. Jemison was one of fifteen people, out of almost 2,000 applicants, chosen for NASA's astronaut training program.

On September 12, 1992, Dr. Jemison and six other astronauts went into orbit aboard the space shuttle *Endeavour*. Dr. Jemison was the first African-American female astronaut. During her seven-day flight, she did experiments to understand the effects of weightlessness. She carried with her several small objects from West African countries. She did this to show her belief that space belongs to all nations.

Dr. Jemison is currently a professor of community and family medicine at Dartmouth College, New Hampshire. She is active worldwide in science literacy and sustainable development. She has founded two companies that are devoted to integrating science and technology into society, as well as an annual international science camp.

---

orbit, a circular path
space shuttle, space vehicle that can fly into space and return to Earth
sustainable development, development that meets present needs without endangering the needs of people in the future

Reading Strategy: Connect Ideas

Circle what Mae Jemison watched on television when she was growing up. How do you think what she saw on television encouraged her to become an astronaut?

Comprehension Check

Circle what Jemison took with her into space. Why did she carry these items with her?

Choose one and complete:

1. Create a cover for a book that tells the secret to success in life.
2. Make a list of five people you would consider to be successful. Then write one question you might ask them to find out how they became successful.
3. Interview a successful person that you know. Ask the person how she or he became successful.

Unit 3 • Reading 1

READING WRAP-UP

Retell It!
Write a summary explaining what the four people you read about had in common.

_____
_____
_____
_____
_____
_____
_____
_____

Reader's Response
What does it mean to be a success? Define your own idea of success.

_____
_____
_____
_____
_____

Think About the Skill
How did connecting ideas between the biographies help you understand them?

_____
_____
_____

Name _____ Date _____

EDIT FOR MEANING

Read
You have read "Success Stories." Now read one paragraph from it again.

Frida Kahlo

At the age of twenty-one, Kahlo met Diego Rivera, a very famous Mexican painter. They got married in 1929. They shared a love of Mexican art and culture. In some of her self-portraits, Kahlo is wearing traditional Mexican clothing and jewelry. In addition to her many self-portraits, Kahlo painted portraits of friends. She is also famous for her still-life paintings—pictures of arranged objects, such as flowers and fruit.

Unit 3 • Reading 1

53

Fix the Error

Each paragraph below contains the same information as the paragraph you just read. However, each paragraph contains one error. First, find the error. Then fix it by editing the sentence so that the information is correct.

1. Find and fix the error.

Frida Kahlo

When she was twenty-one, Frida Kahlo met Diego Rivera, a famous Mexican painter. In 1929 she married him. They both disliked Mexican culture and art. In some self-portraits, Kahlo wears the traditional jewelry and clothes of Mexico. She also painted portraits of friends. Kahlo is famous as well for her still-life paintings, which are pictures of things like flowers and fruit, arranged by her.

2. Find and fix the error.

Frida Kahlo

Frida Kahlo met the Mexican painter Diego Rivera when she was twenty-one. They married in 1929. Kahlo and her husband both loved Mexican art and culture. In some self-portraits, Kahlo wears traditional Mexican clothes and jewelry. In addition to self-portraits, she painted portraits of her friends. Kahlo is not well-known for her still-life paintings—pictures of arranged objects, for instance flowers and fruit.

Name _____   Date _____

FOCUS ON DETAILS

Crossword Puzzle

To complete this crossword puzzle, you'll need to remember or search for details in the reading. Use the words in the word box to help you. Not all of the words in the word box are in the puzzle. Fill in the crossword with answers to the clues below.

Word box:
~~AFRICA~~
EUROPE
MEXICO
MICROCREDIT
ASTRONAUT
EDUCATOR
POLIO
MALARIA
MICROSOFT
ATHLETICS
COMPUTERS
GRAMEEN
BANGLADESH

Across
1. The company that Bill Gates founded
2. Frida Kahlo's native country
4. The continent from which Mae Jemison took many small items when she traveled into space
5. The bank that Muhammad Yunus founded
7. Bill Gates's main interest as a young man
8. Mae Jemison's best-known job

Down
1. The disease that Bill and Melinda Gates want to wipe out
2. Tiny loans to help poor people
3. Muhammad Yunus's native country
6. The disease that caused Frida Kahlo's paralysis

Unit 3 • Reading 1   55

READ for FLUENCY

1. Silently read the text below. Make sure you understand the point that each sentence is making.

2. Underline the word or words in each sentence that are most important. When you read, you should say these underlined words with expression.

3. Look again at the punctuation in the paragraphs. Remember that when a sentence ends in a period, you should read the words as a statement and take a breath before beginning a new sentence. When you see a comma, you should pause briefly. When you see an exclamation mark, you should sound excited. When you see a question mark, you should read as though you are asking a question.

4. Now read the paragraphs below out loud. Pay attention to the important words and punctuation as you read.

5. Write down any words that slowed you down. Practice saying these words out loud.

6. Read the text below out loud two more times. You may want to ask a friend or family member to listen to you and tell you their reactions to your reading.

Muhammad Yunus

In 1974, Bangladesh suffered a terrible famine. Muhammad Yunus decided that it was not enough to teach economics and read textbooks. He needed to do something practical. What if these people were able to receive tiny loans, or microcredit, to improve their situation? Yunus started his project in a small village. He lent $27 to a group of forty-two villagers. They made bamboo stools and bought a cow. And so the Grameen Bank was born.

The Grameen Bank was very different from other banks. First, it provided very small loans. Second, it focused on women borrowers. Yunus believed that women were better at using and repaying loans. Third, only the very poorest people could obtain loans. The system was based on the trust of the bank and the enterprise of the women borrowers. If the borrowers failed to repay, the bank would fail. But it didn't.

Name _____ Date _____

# What defines success?

READING 4: "Students Win Robotics Competition"

SUMMARY Use with textbook pages 176–179.

This newspaper article tells about the successes of the robotics team at Carl Hayden High, an inner-city school in Arizona. In 2004, the team surprised everyone by beating high school and university teams in a national robotics competition. Since then, the robotics team has changed the school and its image. The school is now known as the robot school, and the robotics program has become very popular. Most seniors from the robotics team go to college on full scholarships. The team has not been as successful in competitions recently. However, they have often won awards for helping to get others involved in science and engineering.

Visual Summary

Carl Hayden High School
A school that has turned itself around through robotics

- Students at Carl Hayden High School come from mostly low-income families with little education. Until 2004, the school did not have a reputation for excellence.

- Then in 2004 the robotics team won the National Competition—beating every school and university in the country. Ever since, Carl Hayden High has had a new energy and commitment to excellence.

- The robotics team at Carl Hayden High works hard at winning the National Competition each year. So far they have not repeated their 2004 victory.

  - However, Carl Hayden High has won the Chairman's Award each year: an award for increasing awareness in young people about careers in science and technology.

Use What You Know

List three things you might see at a student science fair.

1. _____
2. _____
3. _____

Text Structure

An article usually begins with a title that tells you what the topic will be. Underline the title on this page. What do you think the article will be about?

_____
_____

Reading Strategy: Ask Questions

You can better understand what an article is about by asking questions as you read. As you read this page, list three questions you want the article to answer.

1. _____
2. _____
3. _____

Students Win Robotics Competition by Karina Bland

**The Arizona Republic
March 15, 2006**

In a stunning upset in the summer of 2004, four inner-city kids from Carl Hayden High won a national robotics competition in California. They beat out high school and university teams from across the country, including the renowned Massachusetts Institute of Technology (MIT).

The school's team of young engineers hasn't done as well since. They came in 26th among 45 teams from across the country, Mexico, and Canada in last weekend's For Inspiration and Recognition of Science and Technology (FIRST) Regional Championship at Veterans Memorial Coliseum in Phoenix.

Still, the winning legacy handed to them two years ago lives on.

The Carl Hayden team earned the top award for their work to get other students involved in engineering and science. It is the only Arizona team ever to win, and now it has done it twice.

Only its robot didn't fare as well. It doesn't seem to matter.

For these teens, there's much more at stake in learning about engineering and building robots than just winning. The 2004 win transformed their school and changed the course of their lives.

---

stunning, surprising or shocking
recognition, special attention
legacy, result of something that happened earlier
fare, manage; succeed
at stake, to be risked

The team has grown from a dozen kids to 50, attracting students from across campus and in different areas of study. It operates like a little corporation promoting a stand-out athletic team, with some students creating brochures, videotaping practice runs or raising money, while others program, design and build robots. Even the cheerleaders come to matches.

"We used to be known as an underperforming school," said Annalisa Regalado, 17. "Now we're known as the robot school."

And now every senior on the robotics team at Carl Hayden in the past three years—about 25, so far—has gone into the military or college, most on full scholarships. All six of this year's seniors are going to college on full scholarships.

Comprehension Check

Underline the passage that tells how the robotics team has grown. Why do you think the team has grown to 50 members?

_____
_____
_____

Text Structure

Articles sometimes include quotations. Circle what Annalisa Regalado says. How do you think this quotation from a student supports the main idea of the first paragraph of the article on page 58?

_____
_____
_____

Reading Strategy: Ask Questions

Underline the sentence that tells what members of the team do after they leave high school. What is one question you might ask these team members?

_____
_____
_____

Unit 3 • Reading 4

Reading Strategy: Ask Questions

Underline the sentences that tell what the robotics competition can be compared to. What might you ask to find out more about how the competition is like these other events?

_____
_____
_____

Text Structure

Articles often have subheadings that are titles for sections of the text. Underline the subheading of this section. What do you think this section of the article is about?

_____
_____
_____

Comprehension Check

Underline the sentence that tells what some students at Carl Hayden are the first to do. What is impressive about this accomplishment?

_____
_____
_____

Success Stories

A robotics competition is as raucous as any football game. There are teenagers in matching T-shirts and hollering parents, teammates and coaches.

"It's NASCAR, science fair and the champion [Phoenix] Suns game all rolled into one," said Allan Cameron, one of the Carl Hayden coaches.

This year's challenge was to design, program and build a robot that could shoot soft foam balls through a hole in a clear plastic wall, like a basketball game for machines.

Carl Hayden's blue robot is "Karen," named after Karen Suhm, a team mentor who has a doctorate in physics. The robot shoots balls off a spinning wheel, like a pitching machine.

"A lot of these kids would have been engineers anyway," Cameron said of Carl Hayden's opponents. "Their parents are engineers or scientists or professors."

But students at Carl Hayden sometimes are the first in their families to graduate from high school, let alone go to college. Now they talk of being computer programmers, engineers and scientists.

Luis Gutierrez, 18, the team's captain, thought he might attend community college.

Annalisa had no intention of going to college. She planned to graduate and get a job, any job. But her teachers have encouraged her to continue her education: "I would feel bad if I didn't go and I let them down."

This fall, both Annalisa and Luis will attend Arizona State University on full scholarships and study engineering.

---

raucous, noisy and loud
mentor, experienced adviser

On to the Nationals

Last year, the teenagers finished third in the underwater robotics competition but edged out MIT again. In last year's FIRST robotics competition, the Carl Hayden kids placed 53rd out of 85 teams.

This weekend's 26th-place finish didn't seem to concern anyone on the team, either, though they wished they had done better.

"Can't win them all," shrugged Fredi Lajvardi, the team's other coach.

What they do keep winning is the Chairman's Award. This is given to teams that increase awareness for science and technology and encourage more children to become scientists, engineers and physicists. It is FIRST's most prestigious team award.

In a year, the students do as many as 45 presentations in schools and to government and community groups. They recently met with Arizona's governor to talk about education policies that could encourage kids to study math and science.

The Carl Hayden kids also mentor kids from 10 junior high schools, helping them build robots and talking about career choices. In December, the students put on the state's annual LEGO competition, recruiting students from the National Honor Society and student government to help.

The robot rests now in a crate, ready to be shipped to Atlanta for the national championship. There, the Carl Hayden kids will face as many as 100 teams with their robot and 30 or so regional Chairman's Award winners for the national title.

---

prestigious, respected as one of the best
recruiting, finding; inviting

Reading Strategy: Ask Questions

Circle the two sentences that tell what happened at last year's competitions. Write one question you might ask the Carl Hayden students about the results of last year's robotics competition.

_____
_____
_____

Comprehension Check

Underline the sentence that explains what the team does concerning the Chairman's Award. Why do you think the Chairman's Award is special?

_____
_____
_____

Comprehension Check

Underline the sentences that explain what Carl Hayden students have done to encourage students to learn math and science. List two ways the Carl Hayden students encourage other students.

1. _____

2. _____

Unit 3 • Reading 4   61

Text Structure

Underline the first highlighted word in this passage. Look at its definition and reread the sentence where it appears. Write your own definition of this word.

_____
_____
_____

Comprehension Check

Circle what the freshmen say about joining the robotics team. How do you think this determination helps the students succeed?

_____
_____
_____

Reading Strategy: Ask Questions

Underline the question at the top of the box on this page. How does asking a question make you want to read the boxed text?

_____
_____
_____

Last year, the team placed second in the national competition for the Chairman's Award.

In August, the team's seniors, like Luis and Annalisa, will leave for college, their spots filled by student protégés from the junior high outreach program. They are 15, freshmen and aware of the legacy they will be expected to carry on.

"We know we have to do well," the freshmen said, both in competition and academically. The boys look at each other and nod. "And we will."

So What Do Engineers Do?

Did you ever wonder what makes a bridge remain standing? Did you ever dream of a car that could run on something other than gasoline? Or ponder how a spacecraft could achieve lift off and then defy gravity and disappear into space? Or wonder how you could actually be safe on a rollercoaster, hurtling through space?

These are the kinds of questions engineers ask. They apply theories of science and math to create practical solutions to real world situations. They make things run faster, slower, higher and safer. They also work to make things more environmentally friendly or more economically sound. Engineers make the world a better and safer place. They change our lives through the innovations they create. Engineering is a growing field, open to almost anyone with the passion and stick-to-itiveness to pursue it.

protégés, young people who are guided by someone with more experience
stick-to-itiveness, ability and desire

Name _____ Date _____

Do Robots Really Exist Outside of Movies and Competitions?

The answer is yes. However, the robots that exist today tend not to be the sophisticated human-like machines we see in movies. Robots like those created by Carl Hayden High are used in factories to do routine or dangerous activity. They're used in situations that people would find too boring, difficult or dangerous. They disarm bombs, are used in space, explore volcano openings or handle toxic chemicals. Robots will increasingly become more complex.

defy, resist or challenge

Choose one and complete:
1. Draw a poster that encourages students to participate in a robotics competition.
2. Write a short play or scene that has robots and human characters. Perform your play in front of the class.
3. Create a model of what your ideal robot might look like.

Use What You Know
What's the name of a movie that features a robot? Describe the robot.

_____
_____
_____

Text Structure
Underline the question at the top of the box on this page. What do you think is the answer to the question? Explain.

_____
_____
_____
_____

Comprehension Check
Underline what the boxed text says about the different ways robots are used now. How do you think robots might help you in the future?

_____
_____
_____
_____

Unit 3 • Reading 4

READING WRAP-UP

Retell It!
Imagine you are a writer for the science section of a local newspaper. Write a short summary of an article you plan to write about a recent robotics competition. Use details from the article you just read.

_____
_____
_____
_____
_____
_____
_____
_____

Reader's Response
Would you like to learn more about robotics? Describe what interests you about robotics and what machine you would like to invent.

_____
_____
_____
_____
_____

Think About the Skill
How did asking questions as you read help you better understand the article?

_____
_____
_____
_____

EDIT FOR MEANING

Read

You have read "Students Win Robotics Competition." Now read one paragraph from it again.

Students Win Robotics Competition

The team has grown from a dozen kids to 50, attracting students from across campus and in different areas of study. It operates like a little corporation promoting a stand-out athletic team, with some students creating brochures, videotaping practice runs or raising money, while others program, design and build robots. Even the cheerleaders come to matches.

Fix the Error

Each paragraph below contains the same information as the paragraph you just read. However, each paragraph contains one error. First, find the error. Then fix it by editing the sentence so that the information is correct.

1. Find and fix the error.

> **Students Win Robotics Competition**
>
> The team has grown from two students to 50, attracting students from across campus and from many areas of study. The team runs itself like a little vacation spot supporting rest and relaxation. Everyone has different jobs. Some students write brochures, while others videotape practice runs or raise money. Still others program, design, and build the robots for competition. Some members also serve as cheerleaders for the team.

2. Find and fix the error.

> **Students Win Robotics Competition**
>
> Students with many different interests have joined the robotics team which has grown from only a few members to more than 50. It is run like a small business that sponsors an all-star sports team. Some students program, design, and build the robots for competition. Others draw brochures, videotape practice runs, or raise money. Everyone is so busy that no one is available to cheer the team on during matches.

Name _____ Date _____

FOCUS ON DETAILS

Word Search Puzzle

To complete this word search puzzle, you'll need to remember or search for details in the reading. Look at the clues and circle the answers in the puzzle below. Check off each clue after you've found the answer. Write the word on the line next to its clue.

1. ✓ A person who studies science _____*scientist*_____
2. ☐ A mechanical invention that performs boring or dangerous tasks _____
3. ☐ A result of something that happened earlier _____
4. ☐ Money given to pay for education _____
5. ☐ The education level after high school _____
6. ☐ To help other students _____
7. ☐ A person who designs and builds roads, bridges, and other objects _____
8. ☐ The study of numbers _____
9. ☐ A group that does something together _____
10. ☐ A place where a person goes to learn _____

O	V	L	J	S	B	W	G	G	H	U	S	E	M	A
S	P	T	M	J	L	E	G	A	C	Y	C	S	E	F
X	C	D	S	A	P	K	Y	G	W	B	Y	K	N	X
A	H	H	K	I	T	A	L	W	E	H	Z	A	T	E
L	X	L	O	R	T	H	K	I	O	Z	F	J	O	N
D	P	V	O	O	A	N	C	X	D	E	E	Q	R	G
Z	O	Y	X	N	L	S	E	O	W	A	N	I	S	I
Y	O	Q	S	W	B	P	X	I	T	E	A	M	E	N
U	H	G	C	Z	H	X	N	L	C	U	O	V	O	E
S	C	H	O	L	A	R	S	H	I	P	L	Z	F	E
J	I	Z	L	G	Q	L	R	V	V	H	I	N	F	R
S	E	O	L	Z	T	A	B	O	S	F	C	K	K	O
T	T	R	E	B	S	O	M	K	B	Y	I	H	K	O
P	C	H	G	T	F	D	V	T	T	O	B	Z	J	V
(S	C	I	E	N	T	I	S	T)	W	G	T	S	M	Q

Unit 3 • Reading 4

READ FOR FLUENCY

1. Silently read the text below. Make sure you understand the point that each sentence is making.

2. Underline the word or words in each sentence that are most important. When you read, you should say these underlined words with expression.

3. Look again at the punctuation in the paragraphs. Remember that when a sentence ends in a period, you should read the words as a statement and take a breath before beginning a new sentence. When you see a comma, you should pause briefly. When you see an exclamation mark, you should sound excited. When you see a question mark, you should read as though you are asking a question.

4. Now read the paragraphs below out loud. Pay attention to the important words and punctuation as you read.

5. Write down any words that slowed you down. Practice saying these words out loud.

6. Read the text below out loud two more times. You may want to ask a friend or family member to listen to you and tell you their reactions to your reading.

Success Stories

But students at Carl Hayden sometimes are the first in their families to graduate from high school, let alone go to college. Now they talk of being computer programmers, engineers and scientists.

Luis Gutierrez, 18, the team's captain, thought he might attend community college.

Annalisa had no intention of going to college. She planned to graduate and get a job, any job. But her teachers have encouraged her to continue her education: "I would feel bad if I didn't go and I let them down."

This fall, both Annalisa and Luis will attend Arizona State University on full scholarships and study engineering.

Name _____ Date _____

Can we see change as it happens?

READING 1: "Changing Earth"

SUMMARY *Use with textbook pages 200–205.*

This passage describes changes that are happening on the Earth as the population, or number of people, increases. As the population grows, people need more natural resources, such as food, water, and fuel. Scientists are working on ways to help farmers produce more food. They are trying to make plants and animals stronger and healthier. Meanwhile, people are also trying to find ways to protect the Earth's environment. If everyone tries to save energy, it will help to save the Earth.

Visual Summary

Risks
The growing number of people on Earth puts increased demands on our limited natural resources, including food and energy.

Solutions
Scientists are using technology to develop ways to provide more food and energy.

Genetic Engineering	**Solar Power and Wind Power**	**Environmentally Friendly Buildings**	**Hybrid Cars**	**Nuclear Power**
Scientists are designing crops so that more food can be produced.	The sun and wind are natural resources that will never run out. Scientists are figuring out how to use these resources to create elecricity.	Architects are designing buildings so that they don't waste limited supplies of energy.	A hybrid car runs on both gasoline and electricity. Driving a hybrid car conserves energy and is better for the environment.	Nuclear power is another alternative, though dangerous, resource for providing energy.

Unit 4 • Reading 1

Use What You Know

List two environmental changes that suggest the Earth is changing.

1. _____
2. _____

Reading Strategy: Scan

Scan the second paragraph to find how many people were living on Earth until the early 1800s. Underline the number. Now scan for and underline how many were living on Earth by 2000. How many more people were living on Earth in 2000 than in the early 1800s?

_____

Reading Strategy: Scan

Scan to find how many more people are alive on Earth each minute. Underline the number. How many more people are alive each hour?

Changing Earth

Growth of Human Population

Earth has changed very quickly over the past 200 years. The human population has grown. Means of transportation have changed. Communication has exploded. People are experimenting with new sources of energy. Even food has changed. What are these changes, and what are their effects?

Until the early 1800s, there were fewer than 1 billion people living on Earth. But since then, improvements in medicine, agriculture, living conditions, and other areas have produced a longer life expectancy and a lower death rate. By 1900, Earth's population had doubled to 2 billion people. The population had grown to 6 billion people by the year 2000. Today, 4.2 people are born and 1.8 people die every second, the United States Census Bureau reports. This means that every minute, 144 more people are alive and living on Earth.

This population growth is increasing the demand for Earth's limited natural resources. These resources include food, water, and fossil fuels. More fossil fuels are needed to power our means of transportation. More food is needed to feed hungry people. And more trees are needed for lumber and paper products.

---

living conditions, food, shelter, and cleanliness of environment
life expectancy, length of time a person or an animal is likely to live

Name _____ Date _____

Society has had difficulty keeping up with the increased demand for resources. When fossil fuels were first used as an energy source, people did not know that burning them could affect the environment. This lack of knowledge, as well as limited technologies, led to air and water pollution. Now, thanks to government regulations and industry efforts, scientists have developed ways to reduce air and water pollution.

Our natural resources are extremely valuable. But they are being used up too quickly. We must be careful not to run out of these resources. The choices we make as individuals, as a nation, and as citizens of Earth all affect the environment.

Food

To feed the world's growing population, scientists have been focusing on ways to increase the food supply. One way is through genetic engineering. In the United States, the government and scientists are working to safely regulate the genetic engineering of various plant and animal foods.

---

society, people in general

Comprehension Check

Underline the sentences that tell what has led to air and water pollution. What are some things people can do to reduce air and water pollution?

_____
_____
_____

Comprehension Check

Restating information in your own words can help you understand a text better. Underline the last sentence in the second paragraph. Write it in your own words below.

_____
_____
_____

Reading Strategy: Scan

Scan for and underline the text that describes how scientists are trying to increase our food supply. Based on what you have read so far, explain why you think it is important to do this.

_____
_____
_____

Unit 4 • Reading 1

Text Structure

A science article often defines key terms and provides examples. Underline the words that define what genes are. Now, list two things about you that are probably determined by your genes.

1. _____
2. _____

Comprehension Check

Underline the part of the text that describes a way scientists are using genetic engineering. In your own words, describe how this will help both farmers and consumers.

_____
_____
_____

Reading Strategy: Scan

Scan for and underline two reasons why genetic engineering may be dangerous. What's your opinion of genetic engineering?

_____
_____
_____
_____

Genes are microscopic structures found in cells of every living thing. These genes determine the characteristics of an animal or a plant. In genetic engineering, scientists put genes from one organism, or living thing, into cells of another kind of organism. One way in which scientists are using genetic engineering is to try to make a plant or animal stronger, healthier, or larger. For example, scientists might insert genes from a certain organism into the cells of tomato plants. This is to enable the plants to survive in very cold temperatures or poor soil. If scientists can produce a tomato that can grow in places where a typical tomato cannot survive, then both farmers and consumers will benefit.

Genetic engineering seems like a good idea to some people. But others say that scientists can make mistakes when changing the characteristics of a plant or an animal. Because this is such a new technology, scientists are not sure yet how genetically engineered plants and animals will affect other living things.

---

determine, control; decide

Another way to increase the food supply is by using chemicals to produce bigger, stronger crops. The most common types of chemicals that farmers use are fertilizers, herbicides, and pesticides. Fertilizers add nutrients to the soil to help plants grow. Herbicides kill weeds. Pesticides kill insects and other organisms that harm plants.

Chemicals can help foods grow and get rid of harmful insects and weeds. But some chemicals can hurt the environment if used carelessly or incorrectly. Certain pesticides, for example, may also kill insects that do not harm crops. They may also hurt the animals that eat the poisoned insects. Scientists test chemicals used in farming to ensure that they meet safety standards. And farmers are trying other ways of controlling insects, such as by adding an insect's natural enemies to fields where crops are growing.

Sometimes the exact source of chemical pollution is difficult to find. When rain or water from sprinklers falls on crops, the water washes away some of the chemicals on the plants. The chemically polluted water then enters the soil and runs off into streams, rivers, and lakes. Runoff also occurs in cities, where chemicals are carried as runoff to rivers and lakes, polluting them.

weeds, unwanted wild plants

Reading Strategy: Scan

Scan for and underline the three most common types of chemicals farmers use. Tell what you think might happen if farmers did not use the chemicals.

Text Structure

Science articles often explain how one event causes another to happen. Underline the sentence that explains how using chemicals can sometimes cause harm. What is one solution to the problem?

Comprehension Check

Underline what the article says about where chemically polluted water can end up. Why is it a problem to have chemically polluted water in these places?

Unit 4 • Reading 1

Text Structure

Science articles have subtitles that help readers know what to expect when they read a section. Circle the subtitle on this page. Based on the subtitle, what did you expect this section to be about?

_____
_____
_____

Reading Strategy: Scan

Scan for and underline the Earth's most valuable fossil fuels. What might happen if these fuels are used up?

_____
_____
_____

Comprehension Check

Underline two everyday examples of ways to preserve natural resources. What's another simple way you can preserve resources?

_____
_____
_____

Fuel Supply

We all use some form of energy in our everyday lives, whether by turning on bedroom lights, using a computer, or riding in a car. Whatever energy we use, the source of that energy is fuel. Oil, natural gas, and coal are Earth's most valuable fossil fuels. The cars we drive depend on these resources. The stoves we use for cooking and many power plants that provide our electricity also need these resources.

Fossil fuels are nonrenewable sources of energy. This means that once they are gone, they are gone forever. Fortunately, there are ways to preserve our natural resources. Everyday choices affect the environment. Something as simple as riding a bicycle to school rather than riding in a car saves energy. Reusing valuable resources by recycling saves energy. Throwing an aluminum can into a recycling bin may not seem very important, but if everyone does it, and does it consistently, it will help Earth.

---

preserve, keep and protect

Name _____ Date _____

Transportation Changes

Scientists are looking for new ways to power cars and other vehicles, such as by using batteries, solar power, and fuel cells. In an all-electric car, a large, heavy battery stores the electric energy that powers the car. When the battery runs low, the driver must recharge it by plugging it into a special electric outlet. Recharging the battery takes much longer than refilling a gasoline tank. Even so, electricity is a relatively clean source of energy for cars, so this extra effort benefits the environment.

Some car manufacturers have developed hybrid cars. These cars run on a combination of electricity and gasoline. Their batteries are small and can be recharged by the car's small gasoline engine while the car is being driven.

Scientists are also experimenting with solar-powered cars and hydrogen-powered cars. Solar-powered cars use solar cells to change energy from the sun into electricity. Hydrogen-powered cars use fuel cells that combine two gases—hydrogen and oxygen—to produce electricity. Solar cells and fuel cells are clean energy sources.

---

batteries, objects that store electricity to power other objects
recharge, put more energy into a battery
engine, machine that makes power from fuel

Reading Strategy: Scan

Scan the first paragraph for three new ways scientists are exploring to power cars and other vehicles. Write them on the lines below.

1. _____

2. _____

3. _____

Comprehension Check

Underline the section of text that tells what a driver of an electric car must do when the battery runs low. Write two reasons why you think drivers might not want to do this.

Mark the Text

1. _____

2. _____

Text Structure

Science articles often provide explanations of how things work. Underline the parts of the text that explain how a hydrogen car battery works. What two gases do fuel cells of hydrogen-powered cars combine?

Mark the Text

_____

_____

_____

Unit 4 • Reading 1

Reading Strategy: Scan

Scan for and underline a benefit of nuclear power. What is another source of energy that shares this benefit?

_____
_____
_____

Text Structure

Science articles often provide definitions of important words. Underline the sentence that uses the word *radioactive*. Rewrite the sentence without using the word.

_____
_____
_____

Comprehension Check

Underline the sentence that describes what the mirrors at a solar power station do. How does the sunlight cause the water to boil?

_____
_____
_____
_____

Alternative Energy Sources

As the number of people on Earth grows, so does the need for energy to make things work. So scientists are searching for alternative sources of energy. One alternative is nuclear power. Nuclear power does not cause air pollution. However, nuclear power must be handled carefully to prevent accidents that could have long-lasting negative effects on living things. That is why strict safety regulations at nuclear power stations are in place. In addition, much of the unwanted leftover material from nuclear plants is radioactive. It can be dangerous for a very long time if disposed of improperly.

Another alternative energy source is solar power. Some solar power stations have hundreds of large mirrors. These mirrors collect and focus sunlight on a large container of water to make the water boil. The boiling water produces steam, which powers machines to produce electricity.

---

radioactive, containing or producing radiation

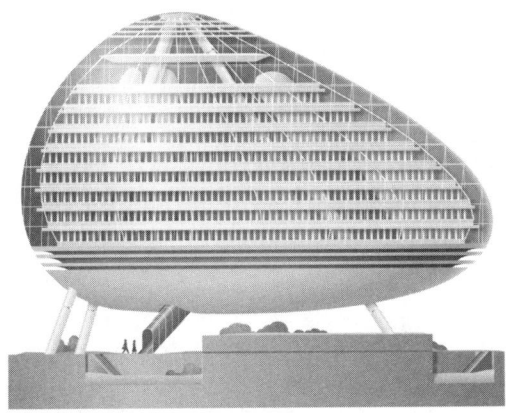

Office building of the future

Wind is also an alternative source of power. People once used windmills to grind grains and pump water. Now wind farms use wind to generate electricity. A wind farm is a large area of land, usually a treeless hill or other windy spot, on which groups of modern windmills operate.

Both solar and wind power are clean sources of energy. They depend on natural forces—sunlight and wind—to work effectively. However, sunlight varies with the weather and the time of day, and wind also comes and goes. Therefore, solar and wind power are not always available to generate electricity.

Environmentally Friendly Buildings

Many buildings waste energy. They use oil, gas, or electricity for heat in the winter and for air-conditioning in the summer. To save energy, many architects and engineers are changing the way they design buildings. The model office building shown here is environmentally friendly. It uses sunlight and ventilation to heat and cool the building efficiently. In winter, warm air at the top heats cold air coming in at the bottom.

---

generate, produce; create
environmentally friendly, not harmful to the environment
ventilation, ways of bringing fresh air into and out of a building
efficiently, without wasting energy or effort

Unit 4 • Reading 1

Comprehension Check

Underline the sentence that tells how wind farms use wind. Write two examples of things that require electricity.

1. _____

2. _____

Comprehension Check
The second paragraph contains the sentence "Both solar and wind power are clean sources of energy." What do you think the word *clean* means in this sentence?

_____

_____

_____

Choose one and complete:

1. Make a chart to show the way our population has grown. Refer to Student Book page 200. Use a ruler—have one inch equal one billion people. Draw vertical lines for each year described. How tall will the line be for the years 1800, 1900, and 2000? Label the lines with their dates and with the numbers they represent. Write a title for your chart.

2. Do an Internet search for insects that destroy food crops. Choose four insects and find information about their natural enemies. Draw a poster about what you find out. Illustrate your poster with pictures of the pests.

3. Draw and label a picture of your dream house of the future. Write about what kinds of energy would keep it warm in the winter and cool in the summer.

READING WRAP-UP

Retell It!

Imagine that you are a television reporter. Prepare a report for the evening news on renewable forms of energy for powering cars and providing electricity and heat for homes. Talk about why these new forms of energy are beneficial. Share your report with others.

_____
_____
_____
_____
_____
_____
_____
_____

Reader's Response

If you could design a house of the future, what would it look like? What kinds of features would it have to help save energy?

_____
_____
_____
_____

Think About the Skill

Did scanning help you find information in the text more quickly? Why or why not?

_____
_____
_____
_____

EDIT for MEANING

Read
You have read "Changing Earth." Now read one paragraph from it again.

Fuel Supply

Fossil fuels are nonrenewable sources of energy. This means that once they are gone, they are gone forever. Fortunately, there are ways to preserve our natural resources. Everyday choices affect the environment. Something as simple as riding a bicycle to school rather than riding in a car saves energy. Reusing valuable resources by recycling saves energy. Throwing an aluminum can into a recycling bin may not seem very important, but if everyone does it, and does it consistently, it will help Earth.

Unit 4 • Reading 1

Fix the Error

Each paragraph below contains the same information as the paragraph you just read. However, each paragraph contains one error. First, find the error. Then fix it by editing the sentence so that the information is correct.

1. Find and fix the error.

> **Fuel Supply**
>
> Fossil fuels are a kind of energy that cannot be renewed. This means that once they are gone, we can get more. Lucky for us there are ways to save our natural resources. We can make choices every day that affect the environment. For example, you can save energy just by riding a bicycle to school rather than driving. When we reuse natural resources, we are recycling and at the same time saving energy. Tossing our aluminum cans into bins that go to a recycling center doesn't sound very important, but if everyone carries out little tasks like that, we can help save our nonrenewable energy sources.

2. Find and fix the error.

> **Fuel Supply**
>
> There is no way that fossil fuels can be renewed. When they are used up, this source of energy will disappear. It is unfortunate that we cannot do anything to preserve our natural resources. Things that we do in our everyday lives can cause effects in the environment. Our everyday choices can make big differences, such as recycling or not using the car for trips that can be made by riding a bike. If we all pitch in, even by tossing aluminum cans in recycling bins, we can do our part to help save the Earth.

Name _____ Date _____

FOCUS ON DETAILS

Mystery Word Puzzle

To complete this mystery word puzzle, you'll need to remember or search for details in the reading. Use the clues to help you unscramble each of the words. Write the words in the boxes. The numbered letters will form the mystery word.

1. Microscopic structures found in cells

    NEEGS | G | E | N | E | S |
                  3

2. A substance that kills weeds

    DICEREBIH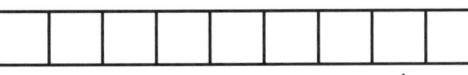

3. A substance that kills harmful insects

    SCDEIPTEI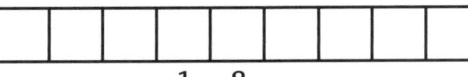

4. A body of information

    GDEEKNOWL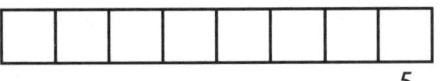

5. A living thing

    NOGRAMSI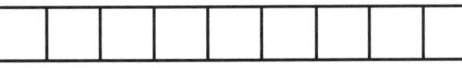

6. A designer of buildings

    TRCIHECAT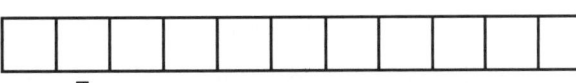

7. Energy that doesn't use fossil fuels

    IVTAELANERT
    [   ][   ][   ][   ][   ][   ][   ][   ][   ]
          7

What is the name of a device that uses wind to produce electricity?

[ ][ ][ ][ ][ ][ ][ ][ ]
 1   2   3   4   5   6   7   8

Unit 4 • Reading 1   81

READ FOR FLUENCY

1. Silently read the text below. Make sure you understand the point that each sentence is making.

2. Underline the word or words in each sentence that are most important. When you read, you should say these underlined words with expression.

3. Look again at the punctuation in the paragraphs. Remember that when a sentence ends in a period, you should read the words as a statement and take a breath before beginning a new sentence. When you see a comma, you should pause briefly. When you see an exclamation mark, you should sound excited. When you see a question mark, you should read as though you are asking a question.

4. Now read the paragraphs below out loud. Pay attention to the important words and punctuation as you read.

5. Write down any words that slowed you down. Practice saying these words out loud.

6. Read the text below out loud two more times. You may want to ask a friend or family member to listen to you and tell you their reactions to your reading.

Alternative Energy Sources

As the number of people on Earth grows, so does the need for energy to make things work. So scientists are searching for alternative sources of energy. One alternative is nuclear power. Nuclear power does not cause air pollution. However, nuclear power must be handled carefully to prevent accidents that could have long-lasting negative effects on living things. That is why strict safety regulations at nuclear power stations are in place. In addition, much of the unwanted leftover material from nuclear power plants is radioactive. It can be dangerous for a very long time if disposed of improperly.

Name _____ Date _____

UNIT 4: Can we see change as it happens?

READING 3: From *Through My Eyes*

SUMMARY *Use with textbook pages 226–231.*

On November 14, 1960, Ruby Bridges became the first African-American student to attend an all-white school in New Orleans. At that time, many areas of the United States had different schools for white and black students. School integration changed that. In this passage, Ruby describes her experiences with integration as a six-year-old girl. She begins by telling about the importance of school integration in the fight for civil rights. Then she tells about why her family decided to send her to the all-white school. She finishes by telling what happened that November morning.

Visual Summary

Ruby Bridges and School Segregation

↓

1954: Supreme Court made it illegal for schools to be segregated. A public school could not turn away a student because of race.

↓

1957: Many Southern states kept their schools segregated even though it was against the law. When nine African-American students entered an all-white public school in Little Rock, Arkansas, they were threatened with violence.

↓

1960: Ruby Bridges, an African-American six-year-old, was the first student of color to attend a formerly all-white public school in New Orleans. So many racist people threatened to harm her that she had to be escorted by federal marshals all year long.

Unit 4 • Reading 3

Use What You Know

Describe what it feels like when you are in a new place and you don't know anyone.

_____
_____
_____
_____

Text Structure

Social studies articles often give information about historic events and their dates. Circle the first year mentioned in this article. What "came knocking" on the door that year?

Mark the Text

_____
_____

Reading Strategy: Draw Conclusions

To draw conclusions, you use all the facts available to you to make a judgment or decison. Underline the word in the second paragraph that suggests that the civil rights movement was a time of great turmoil. Why do you think this was so?

Mark the Text

_____
_____
_____
_____

From *Through My Eyes*
by Ruby Bridges

Preface to My Story

When I was six years old, the civil rights movement came knocking at the door. It was 1960, and history pushed in and swept me up in a whirlwind. At the time, I knew little about the racial fears and hatred in Louisiana, where I was growing up. Young children never know about racism at the start. It's we adults who teach it.

In spite of the aftereffects of the whirlwind, I feel privileged now to have been a part of the civil rights struggle. The 1950s and 1960s were important decades: Negroes, as African Americans were known then, dared at last to demand equal treatment as American citizens. School integration was only part of the struggle, but an absolutely essential part.

---

whirlwind, confused rush
aftereffects, results
privileged, proud; honored
essential, important and necessary

In 1954—coincidentally, the year I was born—the U.S. Supreme Court ordered the end of "separate but equal" education for African-American children. Because of her race, Linda Brown was not allowed to attend her local elementary school. All nine justices of the Supreme Court agreed that Linda had a legal right to go that school. But for a few years afterward, the Court looked the other way when states in the South ignored its order. Black children in states like Louisiana and Mississippi continued to attend all-black public schools. White children went to separate and usually better schools.

By 1957, less than two percent of southern schools had been integrated. That year, nine black high school students enrolled in a white school in Little Rock, Arkansas. The white segregationists in Arkansas were furious. President Dwight D. Eisenhower ordered federal troops—soldiers with rifles and machine guns mounted on military jeeps—to protect the "Little Rock Nine" in their school.

coincidentally, two things happening by chance
enrolled, officially joined

Comprehension Check

Underline the text that describes what kind of education the Supreme Court outlawed in 1954. How was this decision related to the civil rights movement?

_____
_____
_____

Text Structure

Social studies articles often include information about historic locations. Underline the place where nine black students enrolled in an all-white school. How do you suppose they felt on their first day there?

_____
_____

Reading Strategy: Draw Conclusions

When you draw conclusions, use details from the text to support your judgment. Underline details from the text that support the conclusion that the "Little Rock Nine" students faced danger at their new school. Do you think the soldiers made the students feel safer or more afraid?

_____
_____
_____

Unit 4 • Reading 3

Comprehension Check

Underline the sentence that tells what deadline the federal court gave Ruby's city. Why did the court give the city a deadline?

_____
_____

Reading Strategy: Draw Conclusions

What conclusion can you draw about Ruby Bridges's experiences in kindergarten? Underline details from the text that support your conclusion.

_____
_____
_____

Reading Strategy: Draw Conclusions

Underline the words that describe the distance Johnson Lockett Elementary School was from Ruby's home. Did Ruby seem to mind this? Why or why not?

_____
_____
_____

Even after the events in Little Rock, Louisiana continued to ignore its African-American children. However, the civil rights movement was growing stronger. A federal court gave the city a deadline for school integration: September 1960.

I don't remember everything about that school year, but there are events and feelings I will never forget. In writing this book, I recall how integration looked to me then, when I was six and limited to my own small world. However, as an adult, I wanted to fill in some of the blanks about what was a serious racial crisis in the American South. I have tried to give you the bigger picture—through my eyes.

One Year in an All-Black School

When it was time for me to start kindergarten, I went to Johnson Lockett Elementary School. My segregated school was fairly far from my house, but I had lots of company for the long walk. All the kids on my block went to Johnson Lockett. I loved school that year, and my teacher, Mrs. King, was warm and encouraging. She was black, as all the teachers in black schools were back then. Mrs. King was quite old, and she reminded me of my grandmother.

---

deadline, time to end
crisis, turning point; difficult period

What I didn't know in kindergarten was that a federal court in New Orleans was about to force two white public schools to admit black students. The plan was to integrate only the first grade for that year. Then, every year after that, the incoming first grade would also be integrated.

In the late spring of my year at Johnson Lockett, the city school board began testing black kindergartners. They wanted to find out which children should be sent to the white schools. I took the test. I was only five, and I'm sure I didn't have any idea why I was taking it. Still, I remember that day. I remember getting dressed up and riding uptown on the bus with my mother, and sitting in an enormous room in the school board building along with about a hundred other black kids, all waiting to be tested.

Apparently the test was difficult, and I've been told that it was set up so that kids would have a hard time passing. If all black children had failed, the white school board might have had a way to keep the schools segregated for a while longer.

admit, allow to enter

Reading Strategy: Draw Conclusions

Underline which grade level of African-American students would be integrated into the two all-white schools. Why do you think the courts ordered this grade level to be integrated?

_____
_____

Text Structure

Social studies articles can be in the form of a personal narrative, in which the author describes his or her experiences. Underline what Ruby remembers about the day she took the test. Write a memory you have of kindergarten or first grade.

_____
_____

Reading Strategy: Draw Conclusions

Underline the passage that leads you to conclude that the white school board was resisting integrating the schools. Why was Ruby's success on the test important?

_____
_____
_____

Text Structure

Social studies articles often replace long names or titles with shortened forms, called acronyms. These save time and space and make the article easier to read. Circle the letters *NAACP* in the text. What do the letters stand for?

_____
_____

Comprehension Check

Underline the part of the text that describes the benefits of going to the all-white school. List the benefits below in your own words.

_____
_____
_____

Reading Strategy: Draw Conclusions

At this point in the text, what can you conclude about how Ruby's parents felt about her going to an all-white school?

_____
_____
_____

That summer, my parents were contacted by the National Association for the Advancement of Colored People (NAACP). The NAACP is an old and well-respected civil rights organization. Its members work to get equal rights for black people.

Several people from the NAACP came to the house in the summer. They told my parents that I was one of just a few black children to pass the school board test, and that I had been chosen to attend one of the white schools, William Frantz Public School. They said it was a better school and closer to my home than the one I had been attending. They said I had the right to go to the closest school in my district. They pressured my parents and made a lot of promises. They said my going to William Frantz would help me, my brothers, my sister, and other black children in the future. We would receive a better education, which would give us better opportunities as adults.

---

district, particular area of the city
pressured, tried hard to convince
opportunities, chances

My parents argued about what to do. My father, Abon, didn't want any part of school integration. He was a gentle man and feared that angry segregationists might hurt his family. Having fought in the Korean War, he experienced segregation on the battlefield, where he risked his life for his country. He didn't think that things would ever change. He didn't think I would ever be treated as an equal.

Lucille, my mother, was convinced that no harm would come to us. She thought that the opportunity for me to get the best education possible was worth the risk, and she finally convinced my father.

Text Structure

Social studies articles often describe two sides to an argument or conflict. Underline the sentence that tells Ruby's father's opinion about her going to an all-white school. What was he afraid of?

_____
_____
_____

Reading Strategy: Draw Conclusions

Circle the sentence that tells about Abon's experience in the Korean War. What conclusion did he draw from this experience?

_____
_____
_____

Comprehension Check

Underline the two reasons Ruby's mother wanted her to go to the all-white school. In your own words, explain Ruby's mother's opinion about Ruby attending a formerly all-white school.

_____
_____
_____
_____
_____

Unit 4 • Reading 3

Reading Strategy: Draw Conclusions

Underline details from the text about Ruby's trip to school on her first day there. What conclusion can you draw about the level of danger facing Ruby that morning?

_____
_____
_____

Comprehension Check

Underline how far Ruby's new school was from her house. Why do you think they drove instead of walked to the school?

_____
_____
_____

Text Structure

Social studies articles are sometimes written in the first person. This can make it seem as if the author is talking directly to you. Underline the two sentences where the author uses the pronoun *I*. Does this help you understand the author's experience better? Why or why not?

_____
_____
_____
_____

November 14, 1960

My mother took special care getting me ready for school. When somebody knocked on my door that morning, my mother expected to see people from the NAACP. Instead, she saw four serious-looking white men, dressed in suits and wearing armbands. They were U.S. federal marshals. They had come to drive us to school and stay with us all day. I learned later they were carrying guns.

I remember climbing into the back seat of the marshals' car with my mother, but I don't remember feeling frightened. William Frantz Public School was only five blocks away, so one of the marshals in the front seat told my mother right away what we should do when we got there.

---

armbands, bands of material worn around the arm
federal marshals, government officers

"Let us get out of the car first," the marshal said. "Then you'll get out, and the four of us will surround you and your daughter. We'll walk up to the door together. Just walk straight ahead, and don't look back."

When we were near the school, my mother said, "Ruby, I want you to behave yourself today and do what the marshals say."

We drove down North Galvez Street to the point where it crosses Alvar. I remember looking out of the car as we pulled up to the Frantz school. There were barricades and people shouting and policemen everywhere. I thought maybe it was Mardi Gras, the carnival that takes place in New Orleans every year. Mardi Gras was always noisy.

---

barricades, objects blocking a road to prevent people from entering

---

Comprehension Check

Underline the part of the text that describes the plan for getting Ruby safely into the building. Why did the marshals take these precautions?

_____
_____
_____

Reading Strategy: Draw Conclusions

Underline what Ruby's mother told her when they were near the school. Would you conclude from this that Ruby's mother was worried? Why or why not?

_____
_____
_____

Comprehension Check

Underline the details from the text that led Ruby to think that the crowds outside her new school were there for a carnival. How do you think she felt at that moment?

_____
_____
_____

Unit 4 • Reading 3

Comprehension Check

Underline Ruby's impression of her new school. What does this tell you about the difference between schools for whites and schools for African Americans?

_____

_____

Reading Strategy: Draw Conclusions

Underline what the people in the crowd were doing. How would you describe the behavior of the crowd toward Ruby?

_____

_____

_____

Text Structure

Underline the last sentence in the article. What does this sentence tell us about how young Ruby Bridges understood what was happening on that historic morning?

_____

_____

_____

As we walked through the crowd, I didn't see any faces. I guess that's because I wasn't very tall and I was surrounded by the marshals. People yelled and threw things. I could see the school building, and it looked bigger and nicer than my old school. When we climbed the high steps to the front door, there were policemen in uniforms at the top. The policemen at the door and the crowd behind us made me think this was an important place.

It must be college, I thought to myself.

Choose one and complete:

1. Draw a picture of Ruby as she walks into her all-white school on the first day. Draw it as things may have looked to her, as a very young child. Write a paragraph under the picture that describes what Ruby may have been feeling.

2. Write a letter dated 1960 to the all-white school board. In the letter tell why all students, regardless of their race, need to have equal educational opportunities.

3. Write a poem about being brave even in the face of fear. Base your poem on your own personal experiences.

Ruby was special. I wanted her to have a good education so she could get a good job when she grew up. But Ruby's father thought his child shouldn't go where she wasn't wanted.

There were things I didn't understand. I didn't know Ruby would be the only black child in the school. I didn't know how bad things would get.

I remember being afraid on the first day Ruby went to the Frantz school, when I came home and turned on the TV set and I realized that, at that moment, the whole world was watching my baby and talking about her.

At that moment, I was most afraid.

— Lucille Bridges (Ruby's mother)

There was a certain shyness about Ruby. She would appear at the door of our room in the morning and walk in slowly, taking little steps. I would always greet her with a compliment about how nicely she was dressed to help make her feel special as she was, and make her feel more welcome and comfortable. We would hug, and then we would sit down side by side. We had our corner of the room, and it was cozy. I never sat in the front of the classroom apart. If I went to the blackboard, she was always with me.

I grew to love Ruby and be awed by her. It was an ugly world outside, but I tried to make our world together as normal as possible. Neither one of us ever missed a day. It was important to keep going.

— Barbara Henry (Ruby's first grade teacher)

Comprehension Check

Underline what made Ruby's mother feel afraid on the first day Ruby went to the Frantz school. Why do you think she was afraid at that moment?

_____
_____
_____
_____

Reading Strategy: Draw Conclusions

Underline the last two sentences of Ruby's teacher's recollection. What conclusions can you draw about why the teacher never missed a day of school?

_____
_____
_____

Comprehension Check

Underline the sentence in which Ruby's teacher describes how she felt about Ruby. Why do you think she felt that way?

_____
_____
_____
_____

Unit 4 • Reading 3

READING WRAP-UP

Retell It!

Imagine that you have been asked to give a speech about Ruby Bridges to the students in your school. Describe Ruby Bridges's story in the space provided below. Include enough details so that your audience understands how brave Ruby was to go to an all-white school during the 1960s.

_____

_____

_____

_____

_____

_____

_____

_____

Reader's Response

What did you find most interesting about Ruby's experience? Why did it interest you?

_____

_____

_____

_____

Think About the Skill

How did thinking about details in the text help you draw conclusions that otherwise might not have occurred to you? Provide an example below.

_____

_____

_____

EDIT FOR MEANING

Read

You have read the excerpt from *Through My Eyes*. Now read one paragraph from it again.

One Year in an All-Black School

In the late spring of my year at Johnson Lockett, the city school board began testing black kindergartners. They wanted to find out which children should be sent to the white schools. I took the test. I was only five, and I'm sure I didn't have any idea why I was taking it. Still, I remember that day. I remember getting dressed up and riding uptown on the bus with my mother, and sitting in an enormous room in the school board building along with about a hundred other black kids, all waiting to be tested.

Fix the Error

Each paragraph below contains the same information as the paragraph you just read. However, each paragraph contains one error. First, find the error. Then fix it by editing the sentence so that the information is correct.

1. Find and fix the error.

> **One Year in an All-Black School**
>
> Toward the end of my kindergarten year, the city school board decided to test black kindergartners. They wanted to decide which students would attend white schools. I did not take the test. I was so young that I'm sure I didn't have any idea why I was taking it. My mother helped me get dressed up. We took the bus uptown. Then I sat in an enormous room with many other black kids. All of us were waiting to take the test.

2. Find and fix the error.

> **One Year in an All-Black School**
>
> When I was in kindergarten at Johnson Lockett School, the city school board decided to test black kindergartners. They were testing in order to decide who would get to enroll in the white schools. I was only five, but I took the test. I don't remember that day at all. I got dressed up and rode uptown on the bus. My mother was with me. When we got there, we sat in a huge room with about a hundred other black kids, all waiting to take the test.

Name _____ Date _____

FOCUS ON DETAILS

Crossword Puzzle

To complete this crossword puzzle, you'll need to remember details from the reading. Use the words in the word box to help you. Not all of the words in the word box are in the puzzle. Fill in the crossword with answers to the clues below.

EISENHOWER	DISAGREED	EXAM	JOHNSON LOCKETT
SEGREGATIONIST	TEST	LITTLE ROCK	NEW ORLEANS
ARGUED	~~LITTLE ROCK NINE~~	SUPREME COURT	

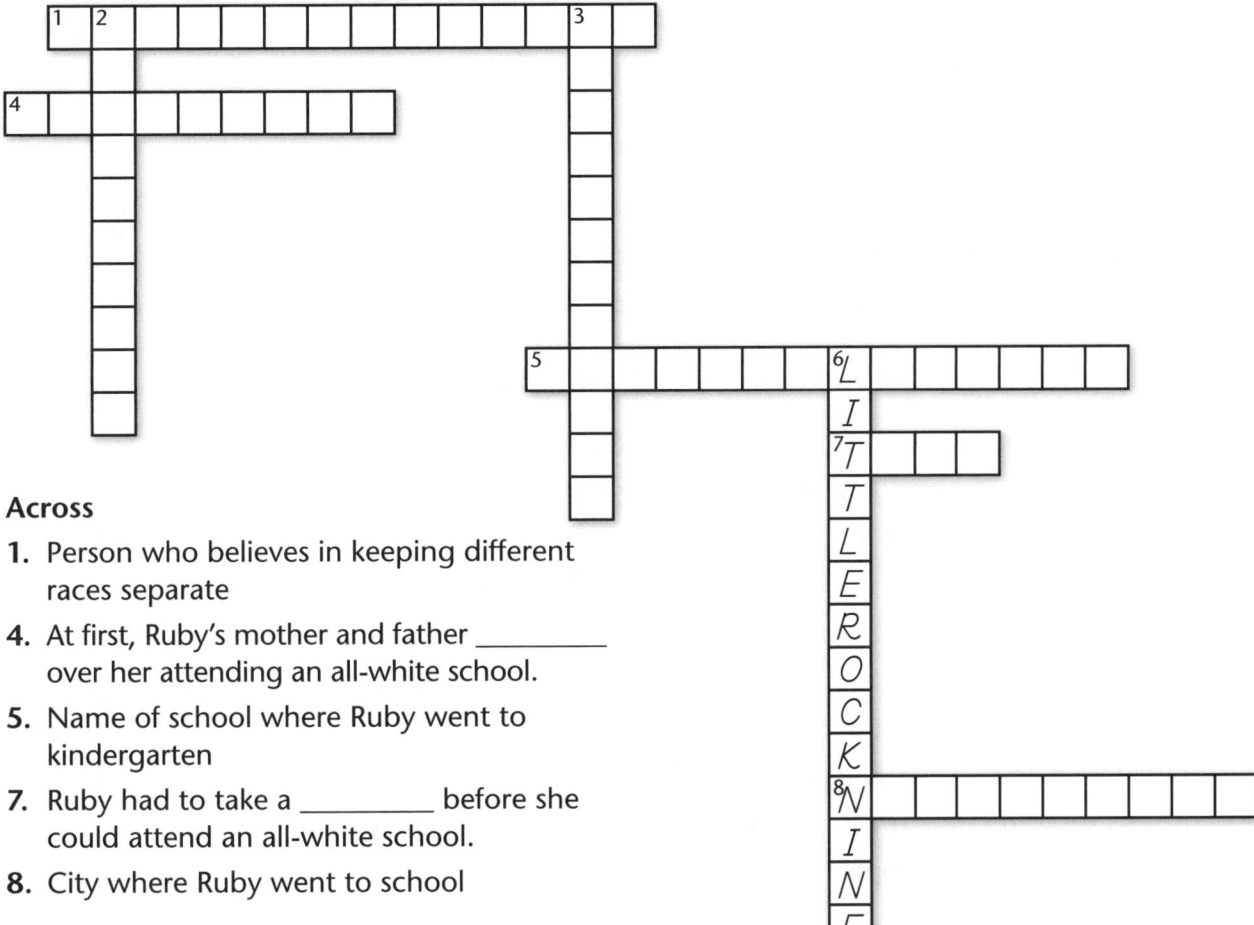

Across

1. Person who believes in keeping different races separate
4. At first, Ruby's mother and father _____ over her attending an all-white school.
5. Name of school where Ruby went to kindergarten
7. Ruby had to take a _____ before she could attend an all-white school.
8. City where Ruby went to school

Down

2. Last name of president who ordered federal troops to help the Little Rock Nine students
3. Government body that ruled in 1954 that the schools had to integrate
6. Name of the first group of students who integrated Arkansas schools in 1957

Unit 4 • Reading 3

READ FOR FLUENCY

1. Silently read the text below. Make sure you understand the point that each sentence is making.

2. Underline the word or words in each sentence that are most important. When you read, you should say these underlined words with expression.

3. Look again at the punctuation in the paragraphs. Remember that when a sentence ends in a period, you should read the words as a statement and take a breath before beginning a new sentence. When you see a comma, you should pause briefly. When you see an exclamation mark, you should sound excited. When you see a question mark, you should read as though you are asking a question.

4. Now read the paragraphs below out loud. Pay attention to the important words and punctuation as you read.

5. Write down any words that slowed you down. Practice saying these words out loud.

6. Read the text below out loud two more times. You may want to ask a friend or family member to listen to you and tell you their reactions to your reading.

One Year in an All-Black School

Several people from the NAACP came to the house in the summer. They told my parents that I was one of just a few black children to pass the school board test, and that I had been chosen to attend one of the white schools, William Frantz Public School. They said it was a better school and closer to my home than the one I had been attending. They said I had the right to go to the closest school in my district. They pressured my parents and made a lot of promises. They said my going to William Frantz would help me, my brothers, my sister, and other black children in the future. We would receive a better education, which would give us better opportunities as adults.

Name _____ Date _____

Why do we explore new frontiers?

READING 2: "Maps and Compasses"

SUMMARY Use with textbook pages 282–285.

This passage tells how to use a relief map and a compass. A relief map shows the geographical features of a region, such as plains, hills, and mountains. Different colors on the map show how many meters or feet an area is above the level of the sea. The scale on a map looks like a ruler and shows the distance between places. A compass is an instrument that shows the location of the North Pole. Compasses were first used over 2,000 years ago by the Chinese and are easy to make.

Visual Summary

Relief Map
Shows geographical features of a region
Different colors show different elevations
Scale shows distances between places

Compass
Shows the location of the North Pole
Helps you figure out what direction you are facing

Unit 5 • Reading 2   99

Use What You Know

List three reasons you might use a map.

1. _____
2. _____
3. _____

Text Structure

A social studies article provides information about subjects related to history, geography, or current events. Underline the title of this article. What social studies subject does this article cover?

_____

Reading Strategy: Take Notes

Taking notes helps you organize and remember the facts you read. Circle two features of relief maps. On the lines below, write what each feature shows.

1. _____
2. _____

Maps and Compasses

Reading a Relief Map

A relief map shows the geographical features of a region. It shows the differences in a region's elevation, or height. For example, by looking at a relief map, you can see whether the land in a region has plains, hills, or mountains.

Relief maps have a key—a box with different colors that show elevation, or how high the land is above sea level. Sea level is the level of the surface of the sea where it meets the land. We measure sea level in meters and in feet.

Maps have scales. The scale on a map looks like a ruler. It shows how many kilometers or miles equal a certain distance on the map. You can use the scale to figure out the distance between places on the map.

---

features, parts
region, particular area
measure, find the size, weight, or amount of something

Name _____ Date _____

Sea level is always 0 on a relief map. Most land in the United States is above—higher than—sea level. For example, the city of Denver, Colorado, is about 1,609 meters (5,280 ft.) above sea level. Dallas, Texas, is about 141 meters (463 ft.) above sea level. Cities that are on a seacoast, such as San Francisco, California, and Boston, Massachusetts, have some land that is at sea level and some land that is higher. San Francisco, for example, is about 20 meters (65 ft.) above sea level in some places. Some land is below—lower than—sea level. For example, Death Valley in California is 86 meters (282 ft.) below sea level.

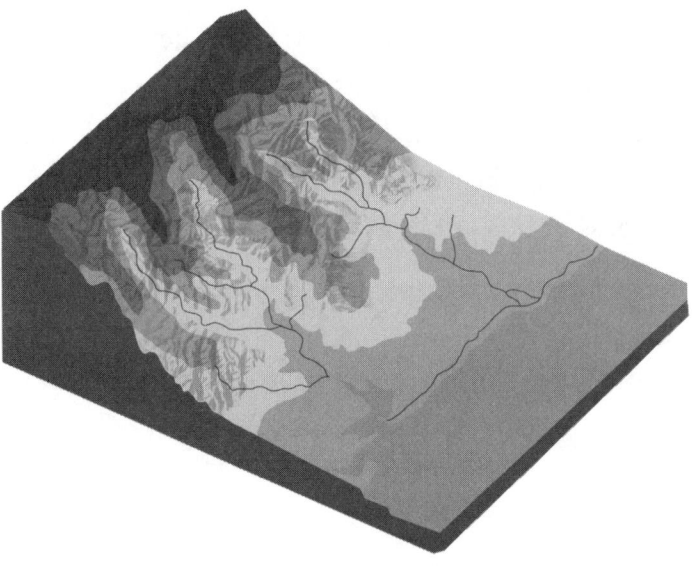

Reading Strategy: Take Notes

Taking note of details can help you remember key points in an article. Underline the sentence that contains the main idea of this paragraph. Then list two locations that are more than 100 meters above sea level.

1. _____

2. _____

Comprehension Check

Underline what the paragraph says about cities that are on a coast. Why do you think coastal cities have some land that is at sea level?

_____
_____
_____

Text Structure

Social studies articles often include numbers or amounts. Circle the highest and lowest elevations listed on this page. What is the difference in elevation between the two places?

_____

Unit 5 • Reading 2

Reading Strategy: Take Notes

When you take notes, you write down important information. Draw a box around the subheading on this page. Write three notes from the first paragraph about the topic of this section.

1. _____
2. _____
3. _____

Comprehension Check

Underline the sentence that tells what a compass does. Why is it helpful to know what direction you are facing?

_____
_____
_____

Text Structure

Social studies articles often define key concepts within the text. Circle the word *lodestone* the first time it appears. How did early explorers use lodestones to make compasses?

_____
_____
_____

The Compass

A map is a useful tool for a traveler, but it does not tell the direction that you are facing. You can find this out by using a compass. A compass is a simple instrument that consists of a small magnet. Anywhere on Earth you can hold a compass in your hand and it will point toward the North Pole. It reacts to Earth's magnetic field.

Over 2,000 years ago, the Chinese discovered a special black stone called a lodestone. The discovery of the lodestone brought about the invention of the first compass.

Early explorers used the lodestone to make their own compasses. They rubbed the tip of a needle against a lodestone to magnetize it. The needle moved toward north. By the sixteenth century, round cards were fixed to the needle. This allowed explorers to take accurate readings from the compass points.

---

magnet, piece of iron or steel that can make other metal objects move toward it
reacts, behaves in a particular way because of what has been done

Name _____ Date _____

How to Make a Compass

You can make your own simple compass.
You will need:

- A sewing needle
- A magnet
- A small cork, or one cut in half
- A plastic container filled with water

1. Magnetize the needle by moving the magnet over the tip of the needle twenty-five to fifty times in the same direction.
2. Carefully push the needle through the side of the cork.
3. Place the container of water on a table or desk. Gently place the cork on the surface of the water.
4. Watch as the needle points north. Now you can determine south, east, and west.

Choose one and complete:

1. Draw a relief map of your schoolyard.
2. Imagine you are going for a hike and using a relief map and compass to keep track of where you are. Write two or three paragraphs about your experience. Tell where you go, what the land is like, and how the map and compass help you.
3. Find a relief map of your state in the library or online. Look at its key. With a partner, design a new key that could be used for the map that uses a different set of colors.

Text Structure

Sometimes social studies articles include guidelines or instructions for completing a task. Draw a box around the bulleted list on this page. How does the list help you make a compass?

_____

_____

_____

Comprehension Check

Underline where you place the cork to make a compass. Why will the cork move easily?

_____

_____

_____

_____

Comprehension Check

Circle the last sentence. How can you determine south, east, and west?

_____

_____

_____

_____

Unit 5 • Reading 2

READING WRAP-UP

Retell It!
Explain, in your own words, what information is shown on a relief map.

_____
_____
_____
_____
_____
_____
_____
_____

Reader's Response
What is the most useful information that you learned about relief maps or compasses in this article? Why was this information useful?

_____
_____
_____
_____

Think About the Skill
How did taking notes help you better understand the article?

_____
_____
_____

EDIT FOR MEANING

Read

You have read "Maps and Compasses." Now read two paragraphs from it again.

The Compass

A map is a useful tool for a traveler, but it does not tell the direction that you are facing. You can find this out by using a compass. A compass is a simple instrument that consists of a small magnet. Anywhere on Earth you can hold a compass in your hand and it will point toward the North Pole. It reacts to Earth's magnetic field.

Over 2,000 years ago, the Chinese discovered a special black stone called a lodestone. The discovery of the lodestone brought about the invention of the first compass.

Fix the Error

Each paragraph below contains the same information as the paragraph you just read. However, each paragraph contains one error. First, find the error. Then fix it by editing the sentence so that the information is correct.

1. Find and fix the error.

The Compass

A map is a useful tool for travelers, but it only tells the direction that you are facing. A compass will also give you this information. A compass is a simple invention that includes a small magnet. The pointer on a compass always points north no matter where the compass is located on Earth. It is controlled by Earth's magnetic field.

The lodestone was discovered 2,000 years ago in China. This special black stone made the invention of the compass possible.

---

2. Find and fix the error.

The Compass

Travelers often find that a map is an important tool. So is a compass. A compass is a device that is made up of a small magnet. No matter where you stand on Earth, a compass always points toward the South Pole. Earth's powerful magnetic field causes a compass to react this way.

The first compass was made possible by the discovery of a special black stone. This stone, called the lodestone, was discovered 2,000 years ago by the Chinese.

Name _____ Date _____

FOCUS ON DETAILS

Word Search Puzzle

To complete this word search puzzle, you'll need to remember or search for details in the reading. Look at the clues and circle the answers in the puzzle below. Check off each clue after you've found the answer.

1. ✓ The height of a region *elevation*
2. ☐ Used, in addition to miles, to measure distances _____
3. ☐ The level of the oceans _____
4. ☐ City that is one mile (1,609 meters) above sea level _____
5. ☐ City on a seacoast _____
6. ☐ Place that is below sea level _____
7. ☐ Where the needle of a compass points _____
8. ☐ What a compass's needle reacts to _____
9. ☐ People who discovered the stone used to invent the first compass _____
10. ☐ A special black stone _____

```
Z R M B I V W S G R Z B R K S
L R X D H F W K F R Z L U I E
M A G N E T I C F I E L D L A
T J X Y X A E R I F E B C O L
H J T S P Z T L G F V I Q M E
J L U I G V O H N X B Z Q E V
B M O O B T K O V W L C R T E
H R J D N O I F E A U O I E L
T O L M E T S S B O L Y V R X
L W I S A S E T G B C L M S W
P O J V Z N T G O U F C E J L
M V E U I O K O P N D T I Y J
I L U H L M C O N G P Z I A G
E N C D E N V E R E Q N R H B
N O R T H P O L E T Y X I K R
```

Unit 5 • Reading 2

READ FOR FLUENCY

1. Silently read the text below. Make sure you understand the point that each sentence is making.

2. Underline the word or words in each sentence that are most important. When you read, you should say these underlined words with expression.

3. Look again at the punctuation in the paragraphs. Remember that when a sentence ends in a period, you should read the words as a statement and take a breath before beginning a new sentence. When you see a comma, you should pause briefly. When you see an exclamation mark, you should sound excited. When you see a question mark, you should read as though you are asking a question.

4. Now read the paragraphs below out loud. Pay attention to the important words and punctuation as you read.

5. Write down any words that slowed you down. Practice saying these words out loud.

6. Read the text below out loud two more times. You may want to ask a friend or family member to listen to you and tell you their reactions to your reading.

Reading a Relief Map

A relief map shows the geographical features of a region. It shows the differences in a region's elevation, or height. For example, by looking at a relief map, you can see whether the land in a region has plains, hills, or mountains.

Relief maps have a key—a box with different colors that show elevation, or how high the land is above sea level. Sea level is the level of the surface of the sea where it meets the land. We measure sea level in meters and in feet.

Name _____   Date _____

Why do we explore new frontiers?

READING 3: "The Cowboy Era"

SUMMARY *Use with textbook pages 294–297.*

This passage tells about the history of cattle ranching and cowboys. Cattle ranching began with the Spanish in northern Mexico and California. Later it became an important part of the Texas economy. In 1866, the first cattle drives began in Texas. Cowboys helped move the cattle north where the animals were sold for high prices. These trips covered long distances and were very difficult. Later, fences were built and railroads came to Texas. Because of this, the cattle drives stopped, and the time of the cowboy ended.

Visual Summary

1845	Texas becomes a state. Cotton and cattle are important to the economy. Some Texas cotton farmers use slaves to do much of the work.
1861–1865	Civil War
1865	Freed slaves join other Texans, becoming cowboys.
1866	Cowboys drive more than a quarter of a million Texas cattle to railroads in Kansas and Missouri for shipping north and east.
1867–1871	Cowboys drive about 2 million Texas cattle up Chisholm Trail to Kansas.
1874	Barbed wire invented; ranges became closed.
1880s	Railroad extended into Texas; cowboys no longer needed to drive cattle to Kansas and Missouri.

Use What You Know

List three things you know about cowboys.

1. _____
2. _____
3. _____

Text Structure

Some social studies articles begin with background information. Circle the date that tells when cattle ranching began in North America. Who were the first cowboys?

_____
_____
_____

Reading Strategy: Summarize

When you summarize, you retell the main ideas of an article in your own words. Sum up the main idea of the first paragraph.

_____
_____
_____

The Cowboy Era

The Vaqueros

Cattle ranching began in North America in the early 1500s. The Spanish settlers brought the first domesticated horses and cattle to Mexico from Spain. The animals flourished and ran free. Huge Spanish ranches were scattered across northern Mexico. The ranchers taught local Native Americans to ride horses and take care of cattle. Often they rode barefoot. These ranchers were called *vaqueros*, from the Spanish word *vaca* for "cow." Ranching spread from Mexico to Texas and California.

Ranches in California

Spanish missionaries introduced cattle ranching to California in the 1700s. Father Junípero Serra established twenty-one missions. Raising cattle became California's main industry. When Mexico declared independence from Spain in 1821, Mexicans of Spanish descent received land grants on which to raise cattle. Some of the ranches were very large—40,000 acres or more.

---

cattle, cows raised on a ranch
domesticated, animals that live or work with people
flourished, grew well
descent, family origin

Name _____ Date _____

Cotton and Cattle

Both cotton and cattle were important to the Texas economy when Texas became a state in 1845. Growing cotton was a lot of work. Most farmers planted and harvested their own cotton. Others were slaveholders, and enslaved Africans did much of the work. After the Civil War (1861–1865), the slaves were freed. Many former slaves became sharecroppers. Others joined the growing number of Texans who became cowboys. They herded cattle on the large, open grasslands, called ranges.

---

economy, a state's or nation's business and money system
herded, moved animals together as a group

Text Structure

A social studies article often has subheadings. Subheadings can signal a change in the topic or a new direction. Circle the subheading on this page. What is a question this section might answer?

_____
_____
_____

Comprehension Check

Draw a box around the name of the plant that was important to the Texas economy. Were most farmers slaveholders? Explain.

_____
_____
_____

Comprehension Check

Underline the passage that tells what happened to slaves after the Civil War. Why were freed slaves important to Texas?

_____
_____
_____

Unit 5 • Reading 3

Text Structure

Social studies articles often include numbers or amounts. Circle the price of cattle in Texas. How much more were cattle worth in the North and the East?

_____
_____
_____

Comprehension Check

Underline the sentence that tells what Texan ranchers realized about cattle. Why was the price of cattle higher in the North and the East than in Texas?

_____
_____
_____
_____

Reading Strategy: Summarize

When you summarize, you restate the main idea and key details. Draw a box around the question at the beginning of the paragraph. What details in the paragraph help answer this question?

_____
_____
_____
_____

Why were cattle important to the Texas economy? Beef was a popular food among Americans. In 1865, people in the northern and eastern United States didn't raise many cattle. Cattle there cost up to forty dollars a head. However, there were more than 4 million longhorn cattle in southern Texas. Cattle in Texas were worth only about four dollars a head. Ranchers quickly realized that they could make a lot of money by selling their cattle elsewhere. First, they could drive the cattle to Kansas or Missouri. There they could ship them to the northern or eastern United States by train. This idea led to the first cattle drives.

---

a head, each animal
drives, acts of herding large groups of animals to another place

Name _____ Date _____

The Great Cattle Drives

In 1866, the great cattle drives began. In that year, cowboys drove more than a quarter of a million Texas cattle through what is now Oklahoma to Kansas and Missouri. This was a journey of about 1,609 to 2,414 kilometers (1,000 to 1,500 mi.), and it took from three to six months to complete. The cowboys and cattle usually traveled on trails that already existed. About 2 million cattle were driven up the Chisholm Trail to Kansas between 1867 and 1871.

Cowboy Life

Cowboys did not have an easy job. Cattle drives were difficult and sometimes dangerous. Cowboys got little pay, worked long days, and got little sleep. River crossings and stampedes were particularly dangerous. Cowboys and cattle might drown crossing a river or get trampled to death in a stampede. Cowboys sometimes had to fight rustlers who tried to steal their cattle.

Some days were scorching hot, and some nights were freezing cold. Cowboys wore practical clothes to help them withstand these temperatures.

---

stampedes, sudden movements of large groups of running animals
practical, useful and sensible

Comprehension Check

Underline the sentence that tells how long the cattle drive took. Why do you think a cattle drive took that long to complete?

_____
_____
_____

Text Structure

A social studies textbook often has highlighted words. Their definitions are at the bottom of the page. Circle the second highlighted word on this page and read its definition. Then rewrite the sentence without using the word.

_____
_____
_____

Reading Strategy: Summarize

A subheading can offer clues to the main idea of a section. Main ideas provide important information to include in summaries. Draw boxes around the two subheadings on this page. Then list the main idea of each section.

1. _____

2. _____

Unit 5 • Reading 3

Text Structure

A paragraph in a social studies article often consists of a topic sentence followed by details. Underline the topic sentence in the first paragraph, and read the details. Now write a new topic sentence for the paragraph.

_____
_____
_____

Comprehension Check

Draw a box around the paragraph that tells about the many ways cowboys used their hats. Why do you think cowboys didn't carry umbrellas, buckets, fans, and pillows?

_____
_____
_____

Reading Strategy: Summarize

Circle three clothing items mentioned in the second paragraph. What details about a cowboy's clothing would you include in a summary of both paragraphs?

_____
_____
_____

Cowboy hats had to be strong and long lasting. On hot days, the high top part of the hat kept the head cool, while the broad brim shaded the eyes and neck. On rainy or snowy days, the hats worked as umbrellas. The hats also protected cowboys from thorns and low-hanging branches. Cowboys even used them to carry water, to fan or put out fires, and as pillows.

The cowboys' other clothing was also practical. Their shirts and pants were made of strong material. They lasted a long time and protected the cowboys' skin. When it was dusty, cowboys covered their noses and mouths with the bandannas they wore around their necks.

---

protected, kept safe from damage or harm

When riding horses, cowboys used their boot heels to prevent their feet from slipping out of the stirrups. When roping cattle, the cowboys could dig their boot heels into the ground.

Many cowboys were native Texans. Others came from the South, East, and Midwest. Some were African-American, Native American, and Mexican. One in four cowboys in the late nineteenth century was African-American. They all had excellent riding skills, enabling them to herd cattle on long drives.

---

stirrups, metal rings where you put your feet when you ride a horse
roping, catching an animal with a circle of rope (lariat)

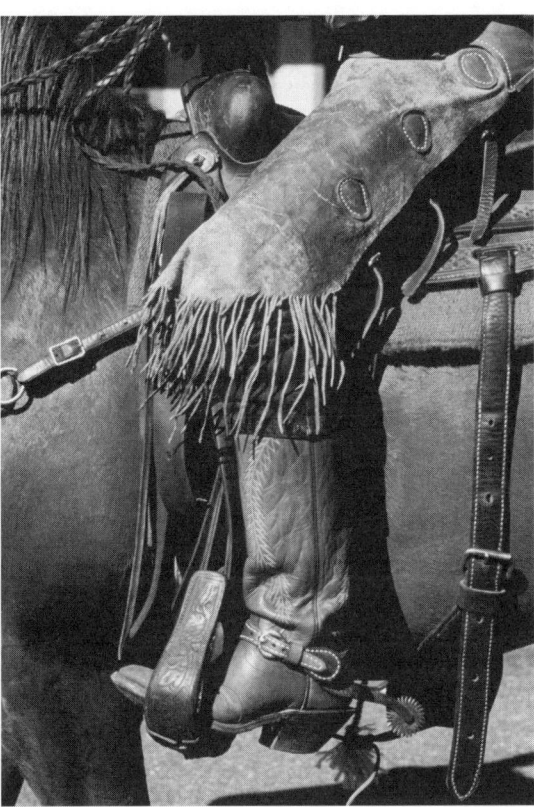

Comprehension Check

Put a check mark next to the paragraph that tells about a cowboy's boots. Why were the heels a useful tool?

_____
_____
_____

Text Structure

Social studies includes not only history, but also geography. Underline where cowboys came from. Which cowboys most likely traveled the greatest distance to reach Texas?

_____
_____
_____

Reading Strategy: Summarize

Circle the second paragraph. Write a sentence that sums up the paragraph.

_____
_____
_____

Unit 5 • Reading 3

Comprehension Check

Underline the topic sentence. Why do you think a cowboy's horse and lariat were his most important tools?

Mark the Text

_____
_____
_____

Reading Strategy: Summarize

When you summarize, you often include several details in only a few words. In your own words, summarize the paragraph on this page.

_____
_____
_____
_____
_____

Text Structure

Underline the second highlighted term on this page. Look at its definition. Then use the word in a new sentence.

Mark the Text

_____
_____
_____

The most important tools for a cowboy were his horse and his rope, or lariat (from the Spanish word *la reata,* meaning "rope"). The lariat is used for catching, or "roping," a cow or steer. It was originally made from braided rawhide, 18 meters (60 ft.) long and about as thick as a pencil. One end was slipped through the honda, or eyelet (made of metal or cow horn), to make a large loop. The honda allowed the rope to slide so the loop could become bigger or smaller. The cowboy held the main line and the loop in his throwing hand, while the rest of the rope was coiled in his other hand, ready to be let out. He also had to hold the reins and steer the horse with that hand. It took a lot of practice to perfect this roping skill.

---

braided, three or more pieces twisted together
coiled, twisted into a round shape
reins, bands of leather around the horse's neck to control it

Name _____   Date _____

End of the Cowboy Era

The golden era of the cowboy lasted only about twenty years. During that time, thousands of cowboys worked on cattle drives. What caused the end of the cowboy era? Until the 1870s, the ranges were open; there were no fences to stop the movement of cattle. However, in 1874, barbed wire was invented. Farmers and ranchers began fencing their land with barbed wire, so the ranges became closed. In addition, many railroads were built in Texas in the 1880s. Then ranchers could send their cattle to market directly by train, so cattle drives became unnecessary.

---

barbed wire, wire with short, sharp points
fencing, building wood or wire structures to stop people or animals from entering or leaving an area
unnecessary, not needed

Choose one and complete:
1. With a partner, write a song that a cowboy might have sung on a cattle drive.
2. On a map of the United States, mark the paths of the great cattle drives.
3. Reread the section "Cowboy Life." Draw a picture of a cowboy, and add labels that explain the importance of each piece of clothing and equipment.

Comprehension Check

Underline the sentence that tells the number of cowboys that worked on the cattle drives. What do you think they did when the cowboy era ended?

_____
_____
_____

Text Structure

Draw a box around the third highlighted term on this page. Look at the definition. Rewrite the sentence without using that term.

_____
_____
_____
_____
_____

Reading Strategy: Summarize

A good way to write a summary is to ask a question about the text and then write an answer. Circle the question in this paragraph. Write an answer to the question.

_____
_____
_____
_____

Unit 5 • Reading 3

READING WRAP-UP

Retell It!
In your own words, explain what the great cattle drives were and why they were needed.

_____
_____
_____
_____
_____
_____
_____
_____

Reader's Response
Explain why you would or would not have liked to have gone on a cattle drive during the cowboy era.

_____
_____
_____
_____
_____

Think About the Skill
How did summarizing help you better understand the article?

_____
_____
_____

EDIT FOR MEANING

Read

You have read "The Cowboy Era." Now read one paragraph from it again.

Cotton and Cattle

Why were cattle important to the Texas economy? Beef was a popular food among Americans. In 1865, people in the northern and eastern United States didn't raise many cattle. Cattle there cost up to forty dollars a head. However, there were more than 4 million longhorn cattle in southern Texas. Cattle in Texas were worth only about four dollars a head. Ranchers quickly realized that they could make a lot of money by selling their cattle elsewhere. First, they could drive the cattle to Kansas or Missouri. There they could ship them to the northern or eastern United States by train. This idea led to the first cattle drives.

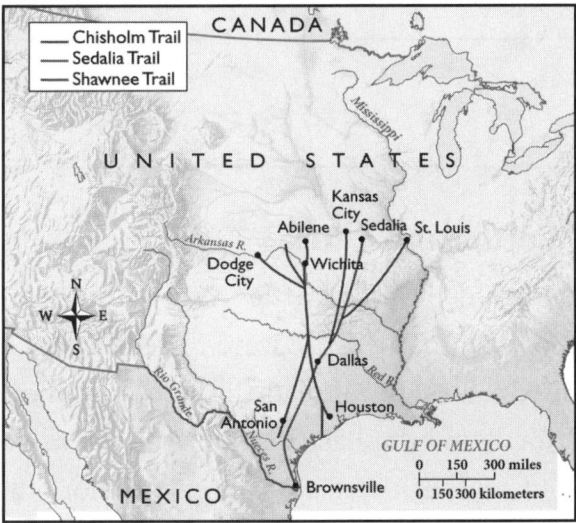

Unit 5 • Reading 3

Fix the Error

Each paragraph below contains the same information as the paragraph you just read. However, each paragraph contains one error. First, find the error. Then fix it by editing the sentence so that the information is correct.

1. Find and fix the error.

Cotton and Cattle

Raising cattle was important to the growth of Texas. That's because many Americans liked to eat beef, but in 1865, people in the northern and eastern areas of the United States didn't have large herds of cattle. Cattle there cost up to a dollar a head. However, ranchers in southern Texas had about 4 million longhorn cattle. The price of cattle there was about four dollars apiece. Texas ranchers thought that they could sell their cattle to hungry northern and eastern buyers. These ranchers decided to move their cattle to railroad centers in Kansas or Missouri. There they could send them to cities in the northern and eastern United States. This plan brought about the first cattle drives.

2. Find and fix the error.

Cotton and Cattle

Why did the Texas economy depend on cattle? Many Americans liked beef. However, in 1865, not many cattle were raised in the northern and eastern United States. Because of the small number of cattle available in the North and the East, cattle were expensive—up to forty dollars each. But southern Texas was home to more than 4 million longhorn cattle. Cattle in Texas were selling for about four dollars each. It didn't take long for ranchers to understand that they could become wealthy if they sold their cattle elsewhere. First, they could drive the cattle to Oregon or Nebraska. Then they could load the cattle onto trains and ship them north and east. This is how the first cattle drives started.

Name _____ Date _____

FOCUS ON DETAILS

Mystery Word Puzzle

To complete this mystery word puzzle, you'll need to remember details from the reading. Use the clues to help you unscramble each of the words. Write the words in the boxes. The numbered letters will form the mystery word.

1. The first cowboys were called this

   ARSEUQOV | V | A | Q | U | E | R | O | S |

                    2

2. Junípero _____ established 21 missions

   RESRA
   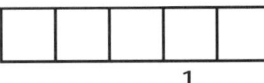
         1

3. Large, open grasslands

   RENSAG
   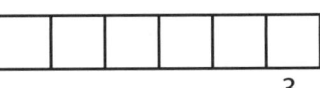
         3

4. How cattle traveled from Kansas or Missouri to the North and East

   TIRNA
   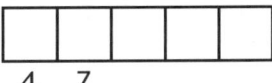
   4   7

5. Trail used by the great cattle drives

   HILSOCHM

            8

6. Cowboys covered their noses with these

   NAASABDNN
   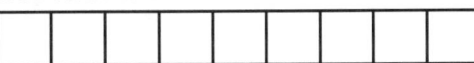

7. Where the cattle started their journey

   ESTAX
   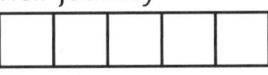
         6

8. The cowboy era lasted this many years

   TWNYTE
   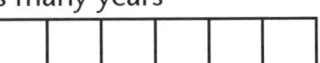

9. The rope used by a cowboy

   LITRAA
   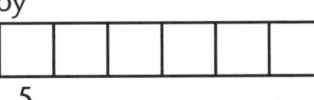
       5

What were the thieves who tried to steal cattle called?

1	2	3	4	5	6	7	8

Unit 5 • Reading 3

READ FOR FLUENCY

1. Silently read the text below. Make sure you understand the point that each sentence is making.

2. Underline the word or words in each sentence that are most important. When you read, you should say these underlined words with expression.

3. Look again at the punctuation in the paragraphs. Remember that when a sentence ends in a period, you should read the words as a statement and take a breath before beginning a new sentence. When you see a comma, you should pause briefly. When you see an exclamation mark, you should sound excited. When you see a question mark, you should read as though you are asking a question.

4. Now read the paragraphs below out loud. Pay attention to the important words and punctuation as you read.

5. Write down any words that slowed you down. Practice saying these words out loud.

6. Read the text below out loud two more times. You may want to ask a friend or family member to listen to you and tell you their reactions to your reading.

Cowboy Life

The most important tools for a cowboy were his horse and his rope, or lariat (from the Spanish word *la reata,* meaning "rope"). The lariat is used for catching, or "roping," a cow or steer. It was originally made from braided rawhide, 18 meters (60 ft.) long and about as thick as a pencil. One end was slipped through the honda, or eyelet (made of metal or cow horn), to make a large loop. The honda allowed the rope to slide so the loop could become bigger or smaller. The cowboy held the main line and the loop in his throwing hand, while the rest of the rope was coiled in this other hand, ready to be let out. He also had to hold the reins and steer the horse with that hand. It took a lot of practice to perfect this roping skill.

Name _____ Date _____

How do we know what is true?

READING 2: "Early Astronomers"

SUMMARY Use with textbook pages 344–347.

This passage tells about some of the first astronomers. By studying how the sun and stars moved, they were able to tell time and direction. They could also count the days and know when the seasons would change. The ancient Greeks were very good astronomers. They named groups of stars after their gods and discovered the planets of our solar system. In the eleventh century, a Persian astronomer named Al-Sufi wrote an important book. It showed the location of stars and planets beyond our own galaxy. Copernicus, a Polish astronomer, suggested that the sun was at the center of our solar system. This was later proven by a German astronomer named Kepler. He also discovered how planets travel in a circle around the sun. Galileo improved the design of the telescope and made important discoveries about the Milky Way and the planets.

Visual Summary

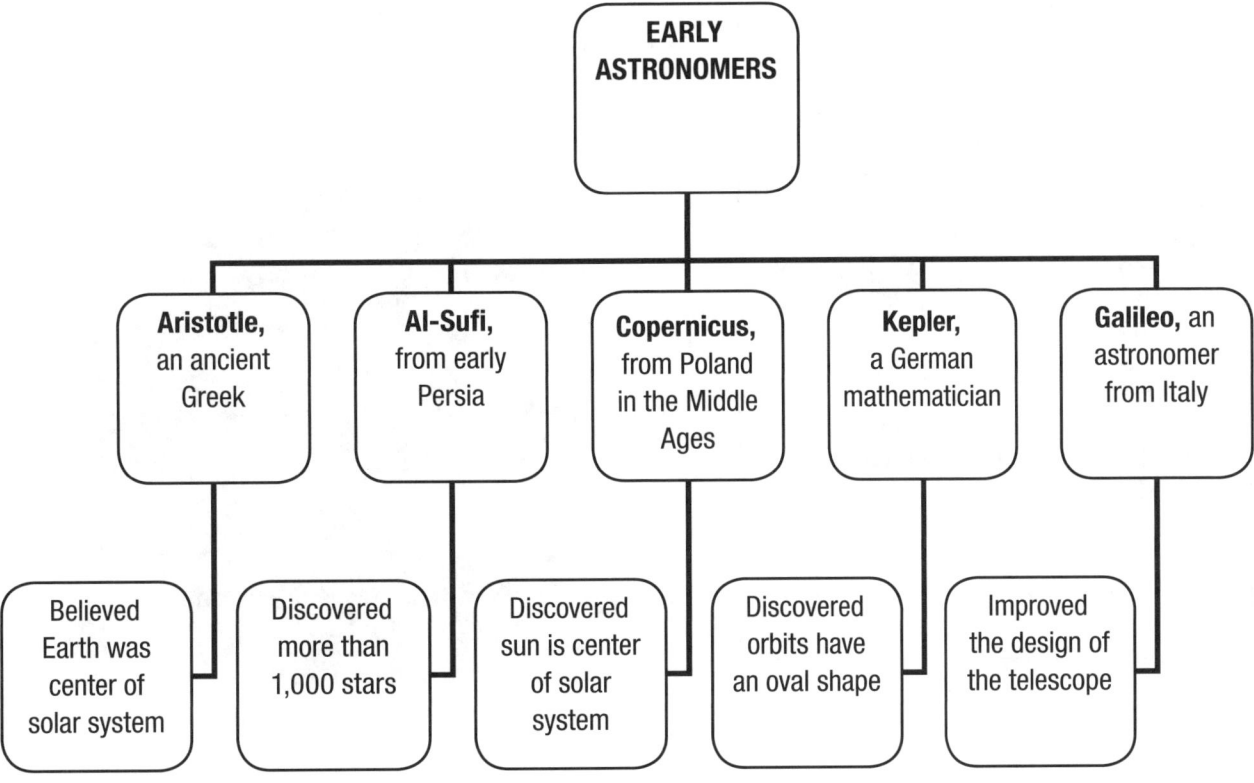

Unit 6 • Reading 2

123

Use What You Know

List three things you might observe in the sky at night.

1. _____
2. _____
3. _____

Text Structure

A science text often has highlighted words. Their definitions appear at the bottom of the page. Circle the second highlighted word on this page. Look at its definition. Then rewrite the sentence without using the word.

_____
_____
_____

Reading Strategy: Evaluate New Information

As you read, you will discover new facts and details. You can evaluate this information by comparing it to facts you already know. Underline what the first astronomers noticed about the night sky. Do you think that what they noticed was important? Explain why or why not.

_____
_____
_____

Early Astronomers

Imagine a time thousands of years ago. You are looking at the night sky. You don't have a watch on your wrist, a map in your hands, or a calendar on your wall. You've never seen a globe or a picture of the solar system. Above you are dazzling points of light scattered across the darkness. You are amazed, but you don't understand what you see.

The night sky fascinated the first philosophers and astronomers. They were intrigued by its beauty and mystery. They studied the sky and made drawings of what they saw. Over time, they began to notice that the points of light moved in regular, predictable patterns. They wanted to identify and understand these points of light and their patterns.

---

globe, ball with a map of the world on it
dazzling, very bright
intrigued, very interested

Name _____ Date _____

People's ability to tell time, count days, predict seasons, and tell direction came as a result of studying the stars. By noting the positions of stars in the sky over periods of time, people developed ways to tell direction. This was very important for nomadic people especially. Noting the changes in the sun's position in the sky enabled people to predict the change of seasons. This was important for people like the ancient Maya. They created their own calendar, as accurate as the one we use today. Having a calendar helped them know when to plant and when to harvest.

nomadic, wandering or roaming

Reading Strategy: Evaluate New Information

Underline things people learned to do as a result of studying the stars. Why do you think it was important for nomadic people to tell direction by studying the stars?

_____

_____

_____

Text Structure

Circle the highlighted word that appears on this page. List two other words for this term.

1. _____

2. _____

Comprehension Check

Draw a box around the ancient people mentioned in this paragraph. How did knowing about the sun and the seasons help them?

_____

_____

_____

Unit 6 • Reading 2

Reading Strategy: Evaluate New Information

Circle the Greek word for *planet*. List one detail you know about the planets. Why do you think learning about the planets was an important discovery for the ancient Greeks?

_____
_____
_____

Comprehension Check

Underline the sentence that tells what names the Greeks called constellations. Why do you think they named the constellations after their gods?

_____
_____
_____

Text Structure

Draw a box around the second highlighted word that appears on this page. Look at its definition. Then rewrite the sentence without using the word.

_____
_____
_____

Aristotle (384–322 B.C.E.)

The ancient Greeks were extraordinary astronomers. They were responsible for many discoveries that form the basis of what we know today. For example, they discovered that some of the bright objects in the sky were not stars but planets. In fact, the word *planet* comes from the Greek word *planetes*. The Greeks also identified and recorded the locations of constellations in the sky. Constellations are groups of stars that form a pattern. Sometimes these patterns look like pictures. The Greeks named constellations after their gods, such as Orion the hunter. They were the first astronomers to name and catalogue everything they could see in the sky.

---

pattern, regular arrangement
catalogue, list

Name _____ Date _____

One of the most famous men of his time was the Greek philosopher Aristotle. His writings covered a wide variety of subjects, such as logic and astronomy. Aristotle believed that Earth was the center of the solar system and did not move. This view of the world lasted for over 1,000 years.

Al-Sufi (908–986 C.E.)

People throughout the Middle East also studied the sky. In Persia (modern-day Iran) during the tenth century, the astronomer Al-Sufi translated many of the Greek works on astronomy. Through his own studies, he located and identified more than 1,000 different stars.

In 964 C.E., Al-Sufi published a book called *The Book of Fixed Stars*. It illustrates the color, brightness, and position of stars in the sky. This book describes a galaxy of stars and planets beyond our own galaxy. Al-Sufi and his work were unknown in Europe. Europeans learned about the stars 600 years later when the telescope was developed.

Comprehension Check

Underline the sentence that tells what the Greek philosopher Aristotle believed. Why do you think that Aristotle's view of Earth as the center of the solar system lasted 1,000 years?

_____
_____
_____

Text Structure

A science article often has subheadings. A subheading can signal a change in the topic or a new direction. Circle the subheading on this page. What is a question this section might answer?

_____
_____
_____

Comprehension Check

Underline the sentence that tells about what illustrations Al-Sufi's book provided. How do you think he learned about the color, brightness, and position of stars in the sky?

_____
_____
_____

Unit 6 • Reading 2

Reading Strategy: Evaluate New Information

Circle the paragraph that tells about Copernicus. Why do you think the Roman Catholic Church rejected Copernicus's discovery about the solar system?

_____
_____
_____

Text Structure

A science article often describes the life and work of an important scientist. When did the astronomer Johannes Kepler live and what did he discover?

_____
_____
_____

Comprehension Check

Underline the last sentence in the second paragraph. How does this sentence illustrate the idea that new discoveries in science are often based on work that earlier scientists have done?

_____
_____
_____

Nicolas Copernicus (1473–1543)

At the end of the Middle Ages, a Polish astronomer named Nicolas Copernicus sparked a revolution in scientific thinking. He believed that the sun—not Earth—was the center of the solar system and that the earth moved around the sun in a perfect circle. The idea of the sun as the center of the solar system contradicted the beliefs of the time, including the beliefs of the Roman Catholic Church. The Church condemned Copernicus during his lifetime, but today he is considered the founder of modern astronomy.

Johannes Kepler (1571–1630)

Like Copernicus, German mathematician and astronomer Johannes Kepler believed that the sun was the center of the solar system. Kepler found the mathematical calculations to support this belief. However, he also discovered that the orbits of the planets around the sun could not be perfect circles, as Copernicus had believed. They had to be elliptical, or oval shaped. Kepler knew from the calculations that this was true, but he didn't know why. The answer came later from the work of the astronomers who followed after him.

---

sparked, activated or set off
contradicted, was the opposite of
condemned, disapproved of

Galileo Galilei (1564–1642)

Galileo, the Italian physicist, mathematician, astronomer, and philosopher, is often called the father of modern science. He asked questions, made observations, and tested his theories. This would later be known as "the scientific method" of investigation.

In 1609, Galileo learned about the invention of the telescope. He improved the design of the telescope so that it gave a much better view of the stars and planets. His telescope magnified objects to thirty times their real size. He discovered that the Milky Way is made up of millions of stars. He also discovered Saturn's rings and Jupiter's moons. Amazingly, no additional moons of Jupiter were discovered until 400 years later, in 2002.

Galileo believed that Earth traveled around the sun. He published his theories and findings in the book *Dialogue on the Two Great World Systems*. Galileo was warned by the Roman Catholic Church to stop teaching his theories, but Galileo refused. He was brought before the Inquisition, a religious court. The court found him guilty of speaking against the Church's beliefs. In 1633, Galileo was sentenced to stay inside his house for the rest of his life.

method, planned way of doing something
warned, told something bad might happen

Choose one and complete:

1. Do library or Internet research to find out more about one of the astronomers mentioned in this reading. Write a one-page biography about his life.
2. Do library or Internet research to learn more about a constellation. Draw and label a picture of it.
3. Imagine you are making a movie about Galileo. Draw a poster for your movie.

Unit 6 • Reading 2

Text Structure

Draw a box around the first highlighted word on this page. Look at its definition. What is another word for *method*?

_____

Reading Strategy: Evaluate New Information

Underline the sentence that explains how Galileo improved the design of the telescope. What are some things scientists can see with today's telescopes that magnify hundreds of times?

_____
_____
_____

Comprehension Check

Circle the sentences that tell what happened to Galileo when he refused to stop teaching his theories. Why do you think he was punished in this way?

_____
_____
_____

READING WRAP-UP

Retell It!
Imagine you are an astronomer who lived after Galileo. Write about his theories and discoveries. How did he improve the work of other scientists? How would you like to continue Galileo's work?

_____
_____
_____
_____
_____
_____
_____
_____

Reader's Response
What did you find most interesting about the early astronomers? Why did you find it interesting?

_____
_____
_____
_____

Think About the Skill
How did evaluating new information help you better understand the article?

_____
_____
_____

EDIT FOR MEANING

Read
You have read "Early Astronomers." Now read one paragraph from it again.

Aristotle (384–322 B.C.E.)

The ancient Greeks were extraordinary astronomers. They were responsible for many discoveries that form the basis of what we know today. For example, they discovered that some of the bright objects in the sky were not stars but planets. In fact, the word *planet* comes from the Greek word *planetes*. The Greeks also identified and recorded the locations of constellations in the sky. Constellations are groups of stars that form a pattern. Sometimes these patterns look like pictures. The Greeks named constellations after their gods, such as Orion the hunter. They were the first astronomers to name and catalogue everything they could see in the sky.

Fix the Error

Each paragraph below contains the same information as the paragraph you just read. However, each paragraph contains one error. First, find the error. Then fix it by editing the sentence so that the information is correct.

1. Find and fix the error.

Aristotle (384–322 B.C.E.)

The ancient Greeks were amazing astronomers. Their discoveries helped form the basis of much of what we know today. For example, they discovered that some of the bright objects in the sky were only stars and were not planets. The Greek word *planetes* became *planet* in English. The Greeks also saw and wrote down where constellations were located in the sky. Constellations are groups of stars organized into patterns that look like drawings. The Greeks named constellations after many of their gods. They were the first astronomers to give names to and classify whatever they could see in the sky.

2. Find and fix the error.

Aristotle (384–322 B.C.E.)

Among the ancient Greeks were some incredible astronomers. Their discoveries helped form the basis of much of what we know today. For example, they studied the nighttime sky and learned that some of the bright objects were not stars but planets. In fact, the Greek word *planetes* changed to become the word *planet*. As they studied the sky, the Greeks also found and recorded where they saw particular constellations. Constellations are single stars with interesting shapes that sometimes look like pictures. The Greeks used the names of their gods to name constellations. They were the first astronomers to record everything they could see in the sky.

Name _____ Date _____

FOCUS ON DETAILS

Mystery Word Puzzle

To complete this mystery word puzzle, you'll need to remember or search for details in the reading. Use the clues to help you unscramble each of the words. Write the words in the boxes. The numbered letters will form the mystery word.

1. People could predict these by studying the stars

    ESSOSNA | S | E | A | S | O | N | S |
                           2

2. The ancient people who created their own calendar

    AYMA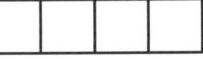

3. A group of stars that form a pattern

    SENCILLONATTO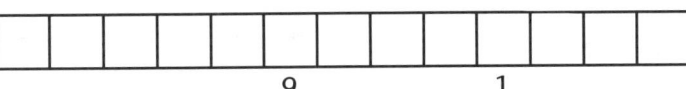
                         9   1

4. He wrongly believed Earth does not move

    REASOLITT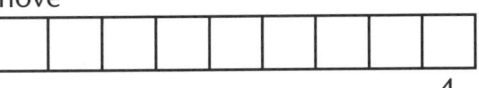
                    4

5. The sun and the planets that travel around it

    LOARS SETMYS
          3

6. A scientist who studies the night sky

    STOAROERMN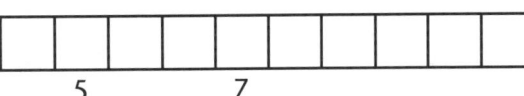
        5   7

7. Oval-shaped

    TEIPILLALC
           8   6

8. This is made up of millions of stars

    LIMKY WYA

9. Galileo discovered the rings that surround this planet

    TUANSR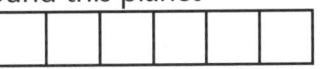

What is a tool you can use to observe the sky at night?

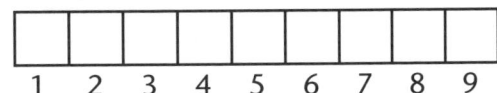
1 2 3 4 5 6 7 8 9

Unit 6 • Reading 2

READ FOR FLUENCY

1. Silently read the text below. Make sure you understand the point that each sentence is making.

2. Underline the word or words in each sentence that are most important. When you read, you should say these underlined words with expression.

3. Look again at the punctuation in the paragraphs. Remember that when a sentence ends in a period, you should read the words as a statement and take a breath before beginning a new sentence. When you see a comma, you should pause briefly. When you see an exclamation mark, you should sound excited. When you see a question mark, you should read as though you are asking a question.

4. Now read the paragraphs below out loud. Pay attention to the important words and punctuation as you read.

5. Write down any words that slowed you down. Practice saying these words out loud.

6. Read the text below out loud two more times. You may want to ask a friend or family member to listen to you and tell you their reactions to your reading.

Early Astronomers

The night sky fascinated the first philosophers and astronomers. They were intrigued by its beauty and mystery. They studied the sky and made drawings of what they saw. Over time, they began to notice that the points of light moved in regular, predictable patterns. They wanted to identify and understand these points of light and their patterns.

People's ability to tell time, count days, predict seasons, and tell direction came as a result of studying the stars. By noting the positions of stars in the sky over periods of time, people developed ways to tell direction. This was very important for nomadic people especially.

Name _____ Date _____

How do we know what is true?

READING 4: "Earth's Orbit"

SUMMARY *Use with textbook pages 372–377.*

This passage tells how Earth moves and what happens when it moves. Earth turns on its axis. An axis is an imaginary line that goes through Earth's center from the North Pole to the South Pole. The turning of Earth on its axis causes day and night. Earth also travels around the sun. Earth's axis is tilted as it moves around the sun. When one hemisphere is tilted toward the sun, there is more sunlight and there are more hours of daylight. This creates summer in that part of the world. The combination of Earth's tilt and its movement around the sun cause the change in seasons. The passage also explains solstices, the longest and shortest days of the year. It also tells about equinoxes, when night and day are the same length of time.

Visual Summary

EARTH'S ORBIT: As Earth moves around the sun, it affects our days, nights, and seasons.

- **Earth's Rotation:** Earth makes a complete rotation once every 24 hours, creating day and night.
- **Earth's Revolution:** Earth makes a complete revolution, or orbit, around the sun once every year.
- **The Seasons** are caused by Earth's tilted axis, which makes hemispheres closer to or farther from the sun.
- **Solstices and Equinoxes:** The longest and shortest days are solstices; equinoxes occur when day and night are the same length.

Use What You Know

List three facts you know about the changing seasons.

1. _____
2. _____
3. _____

Text Structure

A science article often includes subheadings, which can offer clues to the main idea of a section. Draw a box around the subheading on this page. Then write the main idea of the section in your own words.

_____
_____
_____

Reading Strategy: Classify

Classifying facts or details into groups helps you to understand and remember new information. Underline the sentence that tells what an astronomer is. Under what classification would you list planets, stars, and other objects in space?

_____

Earth's Orbit

Earth's Rotation: Measuring Day and Night

The study of the planets, stars, and other objects in space is called *astronomy*. The word *astronomy* comes from two Greek words: *ástron,* which means "star," and *nomos,* which means "a system of knowledge about a subject." An astronomer is someone who studies the stars.

Ancient astronomers also studied the movements of the sun and moon. They thought that the sun and moon were moving around Earth. In fact, the sun and moon seem to move across the sky each day because Earth is rotating, or turning, on its axis. Earth's axis is the imaginary line that goes through Earth's center and the North Pole and South Pole. The turning of Earth on its axis is called its rotation.

---

imaginary, not real

Name _____ Date _____

Earth's rotation on its axis causes day and night. As Earth rotates to the east, the sun appears to move to the west across the sky. It is day on the side of Earth that faces the sun. As Earth continues to rotate to the east, the sun appears to set in the west. Sunlight can't reach the side of Earth that faces away from the sun, so it is dark (night) there. It takes Earth 24 hours to rotate one complete turn on its axis. This 24-hour cycle is called a day.

Earth's Revolution: Measuring a Year

As well as rotating on its axis, Earth is traveling around the sun. The movement of one object around another object is called a revolution. Earth's path as it revolves around the sun is called its orbit. Earth's orbit is not really a circle. It is actually an oval, or egg, shape.

---

faces, points or looks toward
cycle, series of events that happen again and again in a repeating pattern
as well as, in addition to

Text Structure

A science text book often has highlighted words. Their definitions appear at the bottom of the page. Circle the first highlighted word on this page. Look at its definition. Then rewrite the sentence without using the word.

_____
_____
_____

Comprehension Check

Underline the sentences that define a revolution and an orbit.  How are these terms different?

_____
_____
_____
_____

Reading Strategy: Classify

List one detail about Earth's rotation and one detail about Earth's revolution.

1. _____
_____

2. _____
_____

Unit 6 • Reading 4   137

Reading Strategy: Classify

Draw a box around the number of days in a leap year. What is a leap year?

_____
_____
_____

Text Structure

Circle the highlighted term that appears on this page. Look at its definition. Write a new sentence using this word.

_____
_____
_____

Comprehension Check

Underline the sentence that tells the kind of calendar we use. What is the difference between the Roman calendar that we use and the Egyptian calendar?

_____
_____
_____

Earth's orbit around the sun takes about 365 days. In measuring four years of Earth's orbit, three years have 365 days and the fourth year has 366 days. This fourth year with an extra day is known as a leap year. During a leap year, February has 29 days instead of the usual 28 days.

Long ago, people tried to divide the year into smaller parts. They used moon cycles—the time between full moons—as a kind of calendar. There are about 29.5 days between full moons. However, a year of 12 moon cycles, or months, adds up to only 354 days. The ancient Egyptians created a calendar that had 12 months of 30 days each, with 5 days left over. The ancient Romans borrowed this calendar and made changes to it. With more changes, the Roman calendar finally became the calendar we use today. It consists of 11 months of 30 or 31 days each, plus 1 month of 28 or 29 days.

---

full moons, times when the moon looks completely round

Name _____ Date _____

How Sunlight Hits Earth

The equator is an imaginary line around Earth, halfway between the North and South poles. The equator divides Earth into two parts—the Northern Hemisphere and the Southern Hemisphere. It is always cold around the North and South poles and hot around the equator. The warm area around the equator is sometimes called the tropics. Most places outside the tropics have four seasons: winter, spring, summer, and autumn (also called fall).

Why are there different temperatures in different places on Earth? In the tropics, sunlight travels to Earth's surface most directly. As a result, the sun's energy—in the form of heat—is very strong. Closer to the North and South poles, sunlight hits Earth's surface more indirectly—at an angle. Near the poles, sunlight is spread out over a greater area. Therefore, its energy and heat are less strong, and the temperatures are much colder.

---

directly, in a straight line or path
indirectly, not directly
at an angle, not upright or straight

Text Structure

A science article often explains key concepts. Underline the sentence that tells about the equator. What are the two areas above and below the equator called?

1. _____

2. _____

Comprehension Check

Underline the sentence that tells how sunlight hits the North and South poles. How does sunlight that hits at an angle affect the temperature at the poles?

_____
_____
_____

Reading Strategy: Classify

Classify the areas on Earth that are coldest and the areas that are warmest.

_____
_____
_____

Unit 6 • Reading 4

Text Structure

Circle the highlighted word on this page.  Look at its definition. Rewrite the sentence without using that term.

_____

_____

_____

Comprehension Check

Underline the two sentences that tell what happens to Earth's axis for part of the year.
How does the tilt of Earth's axis cause summer in the Northern Hemisphere, and at the same time, winter in the Southern Hemisphere?

_____

_____

_____

Comprehension Check

What season is it in the Northern Hemisphere when the Southern Hemisphere tilts toward the sun?

_____

Why Earth Has Seasons

Why do temperatures around the world change with the seasons? Earth's axis is tilted as it revolves around the sun. The axis always points in the same direction. For part of the year, Earth's axis is tilted away from the sun. For another part of the year, the axis is tilted toward the sun. When the north part of Earth's axis is tilted toward the sun, it is summer in the Northern Hemisphere and winter in the Southern Hemisphere. When the south part of Earth's axis is tilted toward the sun, it is summer in the Southern Hemisphere and winter in the Northern Hemisphere.

---

tilted, with one side higher than the other; leaning

140   Unit 6 • Reading 4

Summer and Winter in the Northern and Southern Hemispheres

In June, the north part of Earth's axis is tilted toward the sun. The hemisphere that is tilted toward the sun has more hours of daylight than the hemisphere tilted away from the sun. The combination of direct sunlight and more hours of daylight creates summer in the Northern Hemisphere. At the same time, the Southern Hemisphere has fewer hours of daylight and indirect sunlight. The combination of indirect sunlight and fewer hours of daylight creates winter in the Southern Hemisphere.

In December, the Southern Hemisphere has more direct sunlight, so it is summer there. At the same time, the Northern Hemisphere has indirect sunlight and fewer hours of daylight. It is winter there.

Comprehension Check

Underline the sentence that tells why the Northern Hemisphere has more hours of sunlight as it tilts toward the sun. How do you think the number of hours of daylight affects what people do?

_____
_____
_____

Reading Strategy: Classify

Classify the times when different hemispheres enjoy summer. When does summer begin in the Northern Hemisphere? When does it begin in the Southern Hemisphere?

1. _____

2. _____

Comprehension Check

Underline the sentence that explains what creates winter in the Southern Hemisphere. What season is it when the sunlight is more direct?

_____

Unit 6 • Reading 4

Text Structure

A science article often explains key ideas or concepts. Underline the sentence that explains latitude. What unit is used to measure latitude?

_____

Comprehension Check

Circle the latitude at the North Pole. Draw a box around the latitude at the equator. Where is the noon sun during a solstice?

_____
_____
_____

Reading Strategy: Classify

What occurs on June 21 in the Northern Hemisphere? What occurs on June 21 in the Southern Hemisphere?

1. _____
2. _____

Latitude and Solstices

Latitude is a measurement of distance north or south from the equator. Latitude is measured in degrees (°) north or south. For example, the equator is at latitude 0°, and the North Pole is at 90° north latitude. On two days each year, the noon sun is overhead at either 23.5° south latitude or 23.5° north latitude. Each of these days is called a solstice.

Each year on or about December 21, the noon sun is overhead at 23.5° south latitude. This is the winter solstice in the Northern Hemisphere and the summer solstice in the Southern Hemisphere. It is the shortest day of the year in the Northern Hemisphere and the longest day of the year in the Southern Hemisphere. Similarly, on or about June 21, the noon sun is overhead at 23.5° north latitude. This is the summer solstice in the Northern Hemisphere and the winter solstice in the Southern Hemisphere.

---

overhead, above your head

Name _____ Date _____

Equinoxes

On two days each year, the noon sun is directly overhead at the equator. Neither hemisphere is closer to or farther from the sun. Each of these days is called an equinox, which means "equal night." During an equinox, night and day are about the same length of time. The vernal equinox (spring equinox) occurs on or about March 21 and marks the beginning of spring in the Northern Hemisphere. The autumnal equinox occurs on or about September 23. It marks the beginning of autumn (fall) in the Northern Hemisphere.

neither, not one and not the other
autumnal, related to autumn, or fall

In about 1500 B.C.E., ancient people in what is now England completed Stonehenge, a giant stone monument. It is thought that they arranged the stones to record the sun's movements, such as the summer and winter solstices and the spring and autumnal equinoxes.

Choose one and complete:

1. Use information from the reading and what you already know to draw a diagram that shows Earth traveling around the sun.
2. Make a poster that encourages people to visit countries in the Southern Hemisphere.
3. Imagine you are preparing to travel to Boston, Massachusetts, and Sydney, Australia, for the month of January. Make two lists to describe the clothing you will need to pack for each place.

Comprehension Check

Circle the date of the spring equinox in the Northern Hemisphere. Underline the date of the fall equinox in the Northern Hemisphere. What is the position of the noon sun during an equinox?

_____
_____
_____

Text Structure

Draw a box around the first highlighted term that appears on this page. Look at the definition. Rewrite the sentence without using that term.

_____
_____
_____

Comprehension Check

Underline the sentence that tells what ancient people completed around 1500 B.C.E. Why might ancient people have wanted to build a monument to record the sun's movements?

_____
_____
_____

Unit 6 • Reading 4

READING WRAP-UP

Retell It!
Imagine you are an author writing a book on the changing seasons. How does Earth's axis affect how the seasons change? When do summer and winter occur in the Northern Hemisphere? When do summer and winter occur in the Southern Hemisphere?

_____
_____
_____
_____
_____
_____
_____
_____

Reader's Response
What did you find most interesting about Earth's orbit? Why did you find this interesting?

_____
_____
_____
_____
_____

Think About the Skill
How did classifying help you better understand the article?

_____
_____
_____
_____

EDIT FOR MEANING

Read
You have read "Earth's Orbit." Now read one paragraph from it again.

How Sunlight Hits Earth

Why are there different temperatures in different places on Earth? In the tropics, sunlight travels to Earth's surface most directly. As a result, the sun's energy—in the form of heat—is very strong. Closer to the North and South poles, sunlight hits Earth's surface more indirectly—at an angle. Near the poles, sunlight is spread out over a greater area. Therefore, its energy and heat are less strong, and the temperatures are much colder.

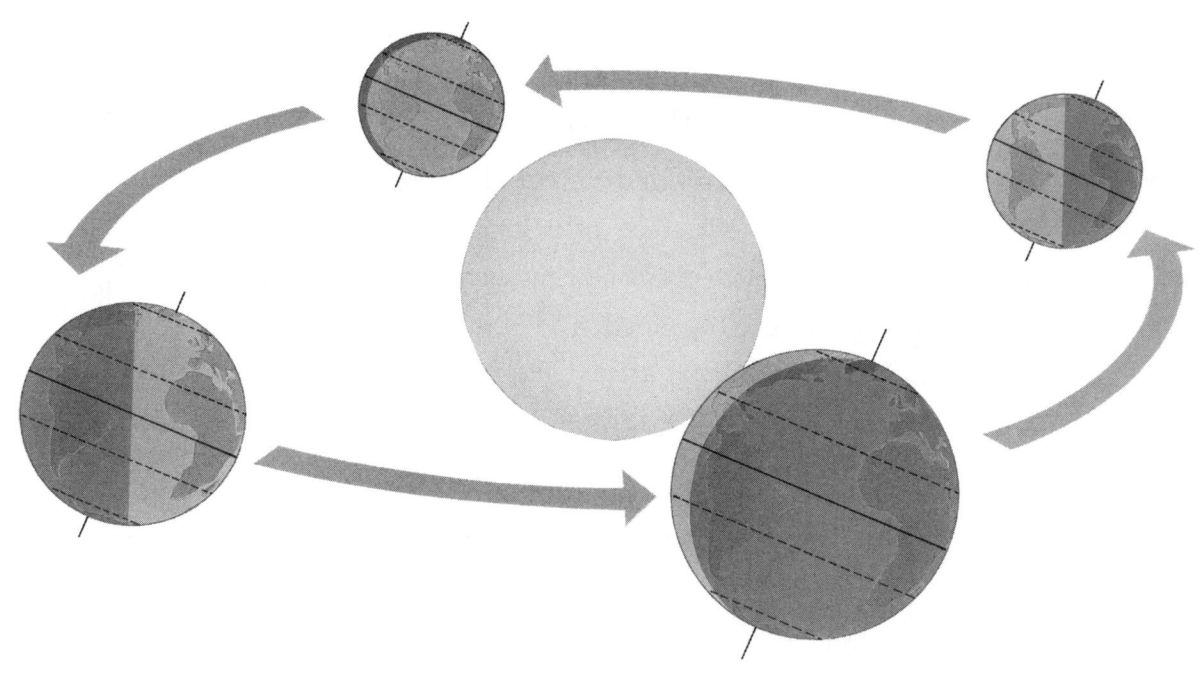

Unit 6 • Reading 4

Fix the Error

Each paragraph below contains the same information as the paragraph you just read. However, each paragraph contains one error. First, find the error. Then fix it by editing the sentence so that the information is correct.

1. Find and fix the error.

> ### How Sunlight Hits Earth
>
> Why don't different places on Earth have the same temperatures? Sunlight hits Earth's surface straight on in the tropics. As a result, heat from the sun's energy is powerful. Closer to the North and South poles, the sun's rays hit Earth's surface at an angle. Near the poles, sunlight is very tightly focused on a small area. The sun's energy and heat are less strong there, which makes the temperatures much colder.

2. Find and fix the error.

> ### How Sunlight Hits Earth
>
> Why are there different temperatures in different places on Earth? Of course, sunlight directly hits Earth's surface in the tropics. As a result, the sun's energy—in the form of heat—is somewhat weak. Sunlight hits Earth's surface at an angle closer to the North and South poles. In those spots, sunlight spreads out over a greater area. Therefore, it doesn't have as much energy and its heat is not as strong, which makes the temperatures much colder.

FOCUS ON DETAILS

Crossword Puzzle

To complete this crossword puzzle, you'll need to remember or search for details in the reading. Fill in the crossword with answers to the clues below.

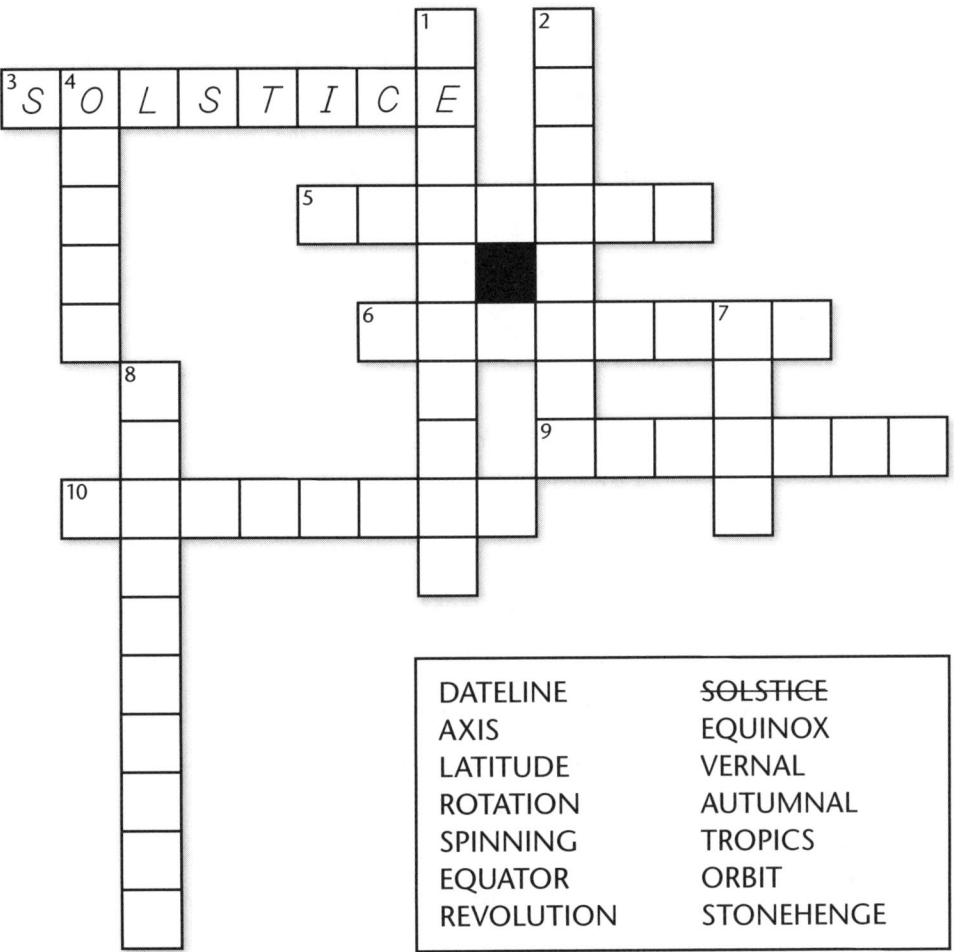

DATELINE   SOLSTICE
AXIS   EQUINOX
LATITUDE   VERNAL
ROTATION   AUTUMNAL
SPINNING   TROPICS
EQUATOR   ORBIT
REVOLUTION   STONEHENGE

Across

3. The shortest or longest day of the year
5. The warm area near the equator
6. Related to the fall season
9. The two times of the year when day and night are the same length
10. The turning of Earth that causes day and night

Down

1. The movement of one object around another
2. Distance from the equator in degrees north or south
4. The path of Earth around the sun
7. The imaginary line that goes through Earth's center
8. A giant stone monument in what is now England

Unit 6 • Reading 4   147

READ FOR FLUENCY

1. Silently read the text below. Make sure you understand the point that each sentence is making.

2. Underline the word or words in each sentence that are most important. When you read, you should say these underlined words with expression.

3. Look again at the punctuation in the paragraphs. Remember that when a sentence ends in a period, you should read the words as a statement and take a breath before beginning a new sentence. When you see a comma, you should pause briefly. When you see an exclamation mark, you should sound excited. When you see a question mark, you should read as though you are asking a question.

4. Now read the paragraphs below out loud. Pay attention to the important words and punctuation as you read.

5. Write down any words that slowed you down. Practice saying these words out loud.

6. Read the text below out loud two more times. You may want to ask a friend or family member to listen to you and tell you their reactions to your reading.

How Sunlight Hits Earth

The equator is an imaginary line around Earth, halfway between the North and South poles. The equator divides Earth into two parts—the Northern Hemisphere and the Southern Hemisphere. It is always cold around the North and South poles and hot around the equator. The warm area around the equator is sometimes called the tropics. Most places outside the tropics have four seasons: winter, spring, summer, and autumn (also called fall).